PRESENTED TO:

FROM:

DATE:

UNBRIDLED FAITH

100 Devotions
from the Horse Farm

CARA WHITNEY

Foreword *by* Dan Whitney,
"Larry the Cable Guy"

THOMAS NELSON®
Since 1798

Published in Nashville, Tennessee, by Thomas Nelson. Thomas Nelson is a registered trademark of HarperCollins Christian Publishing, Inc.

Published in association with the literary agency of WordServe Literary Group, Ltd., www.wordserveliterary.com.

Photos on pages 1, 13–19, 25, 27, 31–35, 39, 43, 47–51, 57–71, 75–89, 93, 97–109, 113–123, 127, 131–139, 143, 147–157, 161–171, 175, 181, 189, 193, 203, 207, and 217 are by Erik Johnson.

Remaining interior images used under license from Shutterstock.

Cover photo by Erik Johnson. Original package design © 2018 Thomas Nelson. Cover design by Halie Cotton.

Thomas Nelson titles may be purchased in bulk for educational, business, fund-raising, or sales promotional use. For information, please e-mail SpecialMarkets@ThomasNelson.com.

Unless otherwise noted, Scripture quotations are taken from the Holy Bible, New International Version®, NIV®. Copyright © 1973, 1978, 1984, 2011 by Biblica, Inc.™ Used by permission of Zondervan. All rights reserved worldwide. www.zondervan.com. The "NIV" and "New International Version" are trademarks registered in the United States Patent and Trademark Office by Biblica, Inc.™

Scripture quotations marked CEV are taken from the Contemporary English Version. copyright © 1991, 1992, 1995 by American Bible Society. Used by permission.

Scripture quotations marked ESV are taken from the ESV® Bible (The Holy Bible, English Standard Version®), copyright © 2001 by Crossway, a publishing ministry of Good News Publishers. Used by permission. All rights reserved.

Scripture quotations marked HCSB are taken from the Holman Christian Standard Bible®, copyright © 1999, 2000, 2002, 2003, 2009 by Holman Bible Publishers. Used by permission. HCSB® is a federally registered trademark of Holman Bible Publishers.

Scripture quotations marked THE MESSAGE are taken from *The Message.* Copyright © by Eugene H. Peterson 1993, 1994, 1995, 1996, 2000, 2001, 2002. Used by permission of NavPress. All rights reserved. Represented by Tyndale House Publishers, Inc.

Scripture quotations marked NKJV are taken from the New King James Version®. © 1982 by Thomas Nelson. Used by permission. All rights reserved.

Scripture quotations marked NRSV are taken from the New Revised Standard Version Bible. © 1989 National Council of the Churches of Christ in the United States of America. Used by permission. All rights reserved.

ISBN-13: 978-1-4003-0331-1

Printed in China

18 19 20 21 22 TIMS 6 5 4 3 2 1

To my Aunt Julie, who shined her little
light into so many dark rooms.
Arnie, Char, and Orlando, for encouraging me to saddle up.
Shirley, for being my role model for gentleness.
Beamon, my spiritual driver.
And to my Little Beedy, for loving us so
well because you love God first.

FOREWORD

I'm sure the first thing you are wondering is, *Why is Larry the Cable Guy, the "Blue Collar Comedy Tour" comedian, writing the foreword to this devotional?*

For starters, my real name is Dan Whitney.

Secondly, the author is the love of my life, my wife, Cara.

I was the son of a preacher and grew up on a farm raising pigs in a small town of 1,200 in southeast Nebraska. I accepted the Lord into my life in my early years, then again in my teenage years, and thirty-seven more times somewhere in between then and now. I was apparently scared of a little cog in life called "hell." I went to church three times a week, attended two Christian schools, and also went to Bible college. Mixed all together, the inevitable result was—*tada!*—me turning out to be a comedian. The Lord blessed me with an outgoing personality and a talent for humor, so I took it and ran with it.

Unfortunately, as the entertainment industry goes, and as the life of an unattached and unaffiliated Christian goes, I became wrapped up in everything this world had to offer. I would have been described as a "backslider." To my regret, I spent too much time away from Jesus Christ. No, I never got to the point where I shunned Jesus or didn't care about the things of God; I was just less engaged in any kind of a walk with Him. Fame, making money, and having a good time crowded out what I knew was best for my soul. Here's the problem with that: a Christian who doesn't stay engaged in God's Word every day and feed his need for spiritual food begins to gradually fall away from God's purpose in his or her life.

This is where my wife comes in.

One night in June of 2003, I met a quiet little lady from a small town in Wisconsin who grew up the same as I did, minus the church activities. Cara wasn't really a religious person, and that would be putting it mildly. She didn't think too much about Jesus or anything spiritual. She actually kinda despised Christians because she thought they were all hypocrites. (All I have to say to that is, "Guilty as charged.")

For sure, I wasn't much good in helping her find the love that Jesus had for her. I was too busy sliding backward down the dark side of Hollywood. But Cara has always been very smart and inquisitive. Every now and then she'd ask me a question about the Bible because she knew I grew up in a Christian home, and she had questions about my real beliefs. The sad shame of it all is that after all my biblical schooling, and growing up how I did, I could barely answer any of them.

In 2005 we got hitched, and then Cara and I were blessed with two kids and a great family. Things were like a fairy tale, and then, *boom*! Health problems hit her and scared us to our knees; we thought she had cancer. It's crazy how a big health scare like running tests for cancer causes you to begin to review your life. It's something God uses to get your attention, that's for sure. He certainly had ours.

Hang with me now. I know I'm more or less telling my wife's story, but it relates to me writing this foreword.

My wife has always been an excellent detective. She's constantly interested in how things work. She's the type who will watch detective shows and try to figure out who did what before the show's over . . . and she's usually right. Well, during her cancer scare, she told God she was gonna search out Jesus and see what He's all about. My wife delved into the life of Christ like Columbo! (He's a TV detective from the seventies . . . tells you what I know about modern shows.)

Anyway, she started reading the Bible and devotionals and doing big ol' Bible study guides. She joined a women's group at the church. She signed up for phone podcasts of pastors and watched videos of apologetics scholars. She bought and ordered just about every learning and study book or CD you can get, including taking an online class at Liberty University. When it was all said and done, her search for Christ had set us back five figures! But the cool thing about it was just like it says in Matthew 7:7 "Ask and it will be given to you; seek and you will find; knock and the door will be opened to you."

Cara had transformed throughout the weeks, months, and years right in front of me into someone who now had peace and happiness. She had a family who loved her, but she also had a deeper joy because of the hope that only Jesus Christ our Savior can give. It was the most incredible thing I've ever witnessed (blowing away Nebraska's back-to-back NCAA football championships in the nineties).

It's amazing to me that I've had this privilege of watching God work in her life. It truly is. When a person opens her heart, seeks the truth, and is truly engaged in the words and teaching of Jesus, the transforming power of the Holy Spirit gives her a peace and a happiness that's unexplainable. My wife is living proof.

While I was watching all this happen, the Lord also began to speak to me. He let me know that I am loved, forgiven, and not ever forgotten. And no matter how many things I've said or done that betrayed who I really wanted to be, or how far away from God I had taken myself, Jesus will always have His arms open to welcome me or anyone else who took a wrong road back into His arms. We are all sinners and have fallen short, but God's grace is free and abundant.

This world is an unforgiving place; the kingdom of God is not. That's why Jesus died for each one of us, and it's why I am writing this foreword. My wife Cara, a petite and shy girl who grew up on a cattle ranch in a town of forty people, not only searched and found hope in Jesus, but has touched everyone's life around her.

Including me. Her husband, Dan.

I'm so proud of my wife, and I hope these devotions will encourage you like they do me. One of her big goals in life is to point everyone she can to the life she has found in Jesus Christ. She's as bold for Christ as anyone I've ever known. She loves people and she shows it by helping folks stay engaged in the good news of Jesus.

Thanks for reading this little foreword, and thanks for reading my wife's book.

—Dan Whitney,
aka "Larry the Cable Guy"

1

WELCOME TO THE BARN PARTY

"Rejoice with me; I have found my lost sheep."
LUKE 15:6

My funny horse is the life of the barn party. His name is Sven, but I call him Fat Benny. He can gain five pounds just by looking at grass (just like my husband with a cheeseburger). He is very vocal, so if he sees me, he will whinny. But as big as he is, his whinny is very wimpy. Fat Benny knows he's fat, so if he wants something on the other side of the fence, he lays on the fence until it collapses and just rolls over the top of it. Benny's antics give joy to everyone at the barn.

Whether it's through your animals, kids, or friends, if you're like me, you find joy in a lot of different ways. However, if you and I want to share the joy of heaven, we need to find our greatest joy in salvation. Jesus told us that there will be "more rejoicing in heaven over one sinner who repents than over ninety-nine righteous persons who do not need to repent" (Luke 15:7).

Our upside-down culture prizes fast cars, expensive clothes, fleeting fame, and shallow relationships over eternal blessings. But as citizens of the kingdom of God, we should put our salvation—and that of those around us—at the top of our lists of things that bring us joy. Think of it: the angels rejoice when one of God's human creations comes to faith in

Him. If you have accepted Jesus as your Savior, the heavenly beings celebrated when you confessed Him as Lord.

There will be a party in heaven for you! Now, doesn't that make you want to kick up *your* heels?

....

Lord, thank You for the gift of salvation—and the great celebration that awaits Your followers in heaven, amen.

2

It's Okay to Not Be Okay

"I no longer call you servants, because a servant does not know his master's business. Instead, I have called you friends."
JOHN 15:15

H orses are amazing animals. When I feel sad or depressed, my horses seem to sense my pain. They turn their ears toward me and even lean into me. In those moments, they aren't just sweet creatures to ride, train, and enjoy; instead, they are my friends.

Still, even if we're surrounded by comforting friends, at some time in our lives, we will be hit with pain so excruciating we will wonder if there is any point in going on. Whether it's a financial crisis, a health catastrophe, or a relationship implosion, our very souls will cry out, "This is too much! I can't live through this!"

Yet with God, we don't have to pretend everything is okay. He longs to be the "friend who sticks closer than a brother" (Proverbs 18:24). He created us, so He knows us better than we know ourselves. We can be honest and real with Him. And His power can help us endure tough seasons. We just have to be humble enough to admit we need Him. You are not big enough to handle life on your own. Run into the arms of a heavenly Father who loves you and weeps with you. Trust Him to be the most loyal, best friend you've ever had.

Lord, thank You for being not only my creator, sustainer, and savior, but also my friend, amen.

3

SILENCE AND PRAYER

Then they sat on the ground with him for seven days and seven nights. No one said a word to him, because they saw how great his suffering was.

JOB 2:13

When I brush my horse, I am really telling him my problems with my hands and my heart. In return, my horse leans into me, seeming to say, "It's going to be okay." By his mere presence, he comforts me. He doesn't have to say a word.

Scientists from England did an amazing study recently that showed that horses know the difference between humans' happy and sad facial expressions and react accordingly.[1] If only we humans were always good at reacting well to our friends' suffering. In the Old Testament, Job was successful and blessed by wealth, friends, family, and stability. Then Satan began to test him, taking away everything—including his health. Job's wife told him to curse God and die. Then his friends came around. Their presence comforted him, and they were great encouragers—until they began to speak, suggesting that Job must have done something sinful to deserve all his suffering. The more they said, the more agitated Job became. Instead of helping him by sympathizing and listening, Job's buddies gave him advice and told him their theories.

Too many times, we are like Job's so-called friends. We are uncomfortable with silence, so we rush to fill gaps in conversation with truisms and opinions. What if we prayed for wisdom before we spoke? It just might make all the difference.

If we wish to be godly encouragers, we must not speak until we have truly listened and prayed. Our words do have a place when we are trying to help someone. But we must let silence and prayer do the talking when we are not sure what to say.

. . . .

Lord, use me to encourage and minister to others—especially those who are hurting. Show me how to be Your hands, feet, and face. Above all, show me how to simply listen, amen.

4

BUCKED OFF OUR HIGH HORSE

Humble yourselves before the Lord, and he will lift you up.
JAMES 4:10

I assumed I knew what my horse Nelson was thinking. Even though I showered him with care, love, and all the things *I* would like if I were a horse, in truth Nelson couldn't have cared less about me. He bucked me off while someone was holding the lunge line. I went on a wild ride, sailing through the air and into the sand, while my friend, who was still holding the lunge line, was dragged across the arena. I was unhurt, but my ego took a beating that day.

On occasion, we all need to be bucked off our high horse. The greatness, forgiveness, and eternal nature of God should humble us. The person of Jesus—His sinlessness, compassion, and self-sacrifice on the cross—should also humble us.

Being humble, for many people, seems like a form of weakness. Pride sneaks in when we start to think we are strong enough to handle things better than God. As believers, we must walk in the footsteps of Jesus and place ourselves under His loving guidance. The Bible has some harsh words about pride: "To fear the LORD is to hate evil; I hate pride and arrogance, evil behavior and perverse speech" (Proverbs 8:13).

Pride is a sin that leads to other sins. When we're filled with pride, too easily we become egotistical and arrogant. However, if we surrender to God daily, asking for forgiveness from our pride, He cleanses us and equips us to deal with life and to love the people around us selflessly. As we walk in humility, we can enjoy the day-to-day release from stress as God intended.

What are you waiting for? Climb off your high horse and fall on your knees before Jesus.

Lord, forgive my pride. Teach me to be humble as I surrender to You daily, amen.

5

THE ONE-TRICK PONY

For I am convinced that neither death nor life, neither angels nor demons, neither the present nor the future, nor any powers, neither height nor depth, nor anything else in all creation, will be able to separate us from the love of God that is in Christ Jesus our Lord.
ROMANS 8:38–39

Horse training is about understanding the horse, not about tricks, food, or force. A good trainer coaxes the horse toward a goal by getting to know the animal first. The trainer gently works with the horse, establishing trust and building the relationship slowly. Bad trainers, however, use fear as a technique. They manipulate and mistreat their horses, believing that domination is the ultimate goal.

In much the same way, Satan uses fear to intimidate and distract us from following God. Our enemy is like a one-trick pony compared to God, but if we allow him to, he can interfere in our lives and wreak havoc on our emotions. Like an abusive trainer, Satan mistreats and manipulates, offering false, right-now rewards in contrast to God's eternal ones. The devil also will do everything he can to trick you into thinking that you're still struggling with something God has already freed you from. Don't give in. During those moments, keep your eyes fixed on the cross and hold tight to the truths found in Scripture.

Nothing can separate us from the love of God. When we confess our sins and trust Jesus as Lord and Savior, we can rest assured that we will spend eternity with Him: "For it is by grace you have been saved, through faith—and this is not from yourselves, it is the gift of God—not by works, so that no one can boast" (Ephesians 2:8–9).

Not only did Jesus give His life so we might know the forgiveness of sin and life eternal with Him, but Jesus also gives us the ability to flee from the devil and have abundant, joyful life here on earth.

....

Lord, steer me clear of the devil's tricks. Thank You for Your gentle leading, amen.

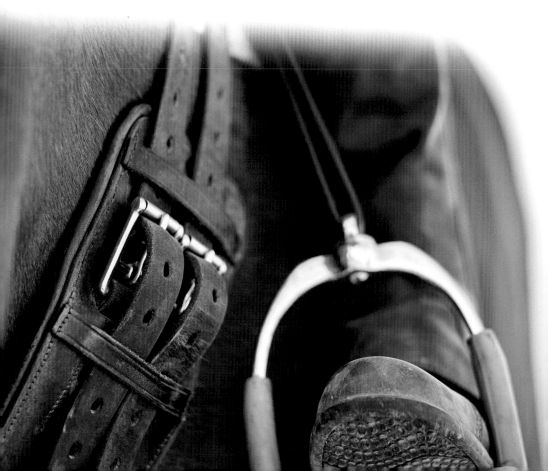

6

———◆———●————————————●———◆———

SKITTISH

When Jesus and his disciples had finished eating, he asked, "Simon
son of John, do you love me more than the others do?"
Simon Peter answered, "Yes, Lord, you know I do!"
"Then feed my lambs," Jesus said.

JOHN 21:15 CEV

Sometimes, I think my horse fears two things: objects that move and objects that don't. In all likelihood, if you look up the word *skittish* in the dictionary, his picture appears next to the text.

And on certain days, I'm skittish too. I trip myself up with doubts and insecurity, and I run away at the slightest provocation. Do you ever have days like that? Fear is a real and powerful force in our lives. It's a force that Satan likes to use to trip us up. The enemy's goal isn't always to hurt us physically, but rather to tempt us to believe that God is not trustworthy.

Peter was one of Satan's victims.

The fisherman-turned-follower-of-Jesus was so afraid after the Lord was arrested that he denied knowing Him three different times. After the resurrection, Jesus met Peter again and asked him if he loved Him. And three times Peter affirmed that he did. After our Lord had destroyed the power of death and had risen from the dead, He stood eye to eye with Peter—giving His disciple a second chance. Once Peter had confessed his love, Jesus assigned him the task of looking out for others. It would not always be an easy job, but as long as Peter released his fear and daily trusted in God, he would succeed.

While the enemy's tactics never change, neither do God's promises. Peter was frozen with fear, but later he was restored to faith. And as we learn from the book of Acts, God used Peter to bring thousands of people to faith—in one day. Satan lost the battle. Is fear pulling you down? Confess it to Jesus and put your trust in Him right now.

Lord, forgive me for the times I have doubted You and allowed the enemy to bring fear into my heart. Empower me to escape that trap and follow You, amen.

7

Salt of the Earth

"You are the salt of the earth."
MATTHEW 5:13

id you know that horses, like people, need extra salt when the weather is hot? And even when it's not hot outside, my horse loves salt.

In Christ's day, salt was a form of currency. It was expensive and hard to obtain. Because Jesus understood the value of salt, He referred to His believers as the "salt of the earth." For us Christians to lose our saltiness means that the gospel has been diluted in our lives. Instead of influencing the world, we let the world unduly influence us. Maybe we quit spending time with God daily and watch too much television instead. Or maybe we focus on all we don't have instead of the gifts God has freely given us. Whatever the specifics, the person who does not protect the biblical truth in her life from the ideas and ideologies of this world will have little flavor left to bless the lives around her.

The truth is, biblically illiterate churchgoers are spiritually immature and vulnerable to anti-Christian teachings and doctrines. Without a firm grasp on the Bible that's nurtured through daily engagement, believers quickly lose their saltiness. They can't stand strong in the faith they claim and are less confident in telling others about Christ.

Life will present you with all kinds of flavors, but it's your salty side that God *loves* most. Get into God's Word—and get growing and witnessing.

....

Lord, I don't ever want to lose my saltiness. Help me to grow
in faith and wisdom, and let my light shine before others,
that they may see Your good deeds, amen.

8

---◆───●──────────●───◆---

WATER CROSSINGS

*"When you pass through the waters, I will be with you; and when
you pass through the rivers, they will not sweep over you."*
ISAIAH 43:2

W ater crossings are not my horse Sven's favorite thing to do. He plants his feet and won't go in. Sven will tiptoe up to it and back, then step left and right. He'll do anything *but* put his foot in the water. I have been told horses have limited depth perception, and they can't tell how deep water is unless they go in. In that case, maybe I need to be working on our trust issues instead. Sven needs to have confidence that I won't ask him to cross where it's not safe to go.

Throughout our lifetimes, you and I will face countless situations where we're not sure it's safe. Some obstacles will be tougher than others, and some will seem downright impossible to overcome.

God will not put an obstacle or situation in front of you that He can't handle. Better yet, God promises to be with you over, around, and through all of them. As Psalm 23:4 says, "Even though I walk through the darkest valley, I will fear no evil, for you are with me; your rod and your staff, they comfort me."

If you have trust issues, take the first step by submerging yourself in God's Word today. The real enjoyment in life and in faith comes when we are willing to get our feet wet. Then take your cries and prayers to

Jesus, who with His eternal power will keep your head above the troubled waters of this world.

....

Lord, give me the strength to handle the obstacles in my life. As I pass through the waters, I will trust that You are with me—just as Your Word promises, amen.

9

One of a Kind

God has also given each of us different gifts to use. If we can prophesy,
we should do it according to the amount of faith we have. If we can
serve others, we should serve. If we can teach, we should teach.
Romans 12:6–7 cev

We all have our opinions on what horse breed is best. God designed each breed differently, from Shetlands to Clydesdales. All of them are exceptional, but none have the same personalities, talents, or abilities. For instance, Fjords and Shetlands have a pony personality. Ponies are like boys—they can be naughty, for sure, but when they see you've reached your limits, they switch gears into charming mode. Even though ponies might have big personalities, by definition they are tiny. You would never ask or expect a Shetland pony to pull a heavy wagon.

Like the many differences between horse breeds, there is a huge diversity of God-given gifts in the body of Christ (the church). The Creator gives each of us a unique personality and talents in order to serve Him, and there is no reason for you to think more highly or more lowly of your gifts than you ought to. After all, you are a one-of-a-kind masterpiece, the very workmanship of God (Ephesians 2:10), knit together in your mother's womb, fearfully and wonderfully made (Psalm 139:13–14).

Whether you teach, preach, encourage, or minister, you are unique. You have been fashioned and equipped by a loving God. He gave *you* the gift of eternal life through Jesus and the opportunities to tell the world the good news. Don't waste a moment more! Get out there and use your God-given talents today.

....

Lord, I praise You and thank You for giving me one-of-a-kind talents and gifts. Help me use them for You and use them well, amen.

10

STAND STRONG

*No temptation has overtaken you except what is common to
mankind. And God is faithful; he will not let you be tempted
beyond what you can bear. But when you are tempted, he
will also provide a way out so that you can endure it.*

1 CORINTHIANS 10:13

During trail rides, Sven has perfected a trick I like to refer to as the
"sneak and eat." When he thinks no one is looking, Sven grabs the
first green thing he sees and tries to eat it. No matter the consequence,
the temptation is just too much. The next thing you know, he'll have an
entire branch sticking out of the sides of his mouth.

We can all relate to temptation. The first man and woman, Adam
and Eve, fell into sin after they were tempted, and they lived in a picture-
perfect environment. Even Jesus was tempted, although He did not sin.

Thankfully, God does not allow His children to be tempted beyond
the borders of their limitations. The fact is, we *will* wrestle with sin in
this life, and we won't experience its complete vanquishing until we meet
the Lord in heaven. However—and this is important—because of what
Jesus has accomplished for us, we are no longer slaves to sin (Romans
6:13–14).

The next time you feel tempted to sin, ask God for help to overcome
it. What's more, ask Him what to do *before* you get tempted. Maybe you

need more rest, a change of scenery, or different social relationships or settings. When He gives you answers, follow through on cutting out negative influences.

Although no one should ever underestimate the power of the devil, God is greater. He doesn't promise that the choice to overcome temptation will be easy, but if you ask for His help, He will give you the strength to stand strong, and the enemy will flee.

Lord, protect me from the enemy and give me the power to withstand temptation. I want to know, love, serve, and follow You, amen.

11

SET FREE

Blessed is he whose transgression is forgiven, whose sin is covered. Blessed is the man to whom the LORD does not impute iniquity, and in whose spirit there is no deceit.
PSALM 32:1–2 NKJV

It doesn't matter how much we want to continue riding, trying to push an exhausted horse farther is not going to get us anywhere. I've learned the hard way: it's always best to end the ride on a high note. If I sense my horse's patience growing shorter, I need to stop for the day. Otherwise, my repeated efforts to get somewhere will be wasted.

In much the same way, do you find yourself repeatedly asking God to forgive you for something He has already forgiven? If you have already accepted Jesus as your Savior and repented of your sin, that sin is forgiven, period.

Perhaps the answer is learning *how* to forgive ourselves. When we sin, one simple prayer of true repentance may seem too easy. But it's not. It's the devil who causes us to think more about our sin than our Savior.

As we give in to doubt and relive a past sin, the enemy sees a foothold. But during our weak moments, we can choose whether we are going to believe God or the devil. If we trade self-confidence for God confidence, it will change our lives. "Let us then approach God's throne of grace with confidence, so that we may receive mercy and find grace to help us in our time of need" (Hebrews 4:16).

Christ already paid the price for our sins when He submitted to death on a cross. Colossians 2:13–14 says: "He forgave us all our sins, having canceled the charge of our legal indebtedness, which stood against us and condemned us; he has taken it away, nailing it to the cross."

Until you let go of your past and learn to trust God's love and forgiveness, you will never leave the stall. No sin is beyond the Almighty's ability to forgive. Trust in Him. He has already set you free.

....

Lord, I praise You that my sin is covered. I don't have to relive the past. Help me to trust Your love and forgiveness, amen.

12

TOO MANY TREATS

Trust GOD from the bottom of your heart.
PROVERBS 3:5, THE MESSAGE

It's tough to say no to my pony, Tucker, when he wants a treat.
I bet you're familiar with the look ponies give their owners: sad eyes, followed by all that nickering for our attention. I used to give in to this—every time. But I ended up giving Tucker so many treats that I made him sick. After that, I became wiser about what I gave him, and he was healthier for it.

Like Tucker, we're often incapable of knowing which things will truly make us happy. If God were to grant us our every wish, more than likely He would end up doing us more harm than good. Fortunately for us, God is not only a Provider, but a Father we can trust to discern what's really good for us.

There's a hit by Garth Brooks from the nineties called "Unanswered Prayers." In the song, he runs into an old high school crush at a football game. Suddenly, Garth remembers praying daily for that girl to be his. At the time, he was devastated by their eventual breakup, but with the benefit of hindsight, the singer realizes how God had protected him. "I guess the Lord knows what he's doin' after all," Garth sings.

Thank God today for protecting you from "that thing" you were convinced you had to have. Then praise Him for blessing you with the thing He knew you needed.

....

Lord, thank You for knowing what's best and giving me what I need, not always what I want. Help me to trust You from the bottom of my heart, amen.

13

A Lesson from a Horse

*"So watch yourselves. If your brother or sister sins against
you, rebuke them; and if they repent, forgive them. Even if
they sin against you seven times in a day and seven times come
back to you saying 'I repent,' you must forgive them."*
LUKE 17:3–4

Ramming our feet into the stirrups. Pulling on our horses' mouths
with the reins. Losing our tempers. It's nice to know that horses
forgive us. A few times, I have accused a horse of naughtiness, only to
discover later that he was actually reacting to something painful. I have
lost my temper and fussed at horses. I accidentally hit one with a rope
and unintentionally hit another in the face with a gate while opening
it. Thank goodness they were not injured, but I felt terrible nonetheless.

The truth is, horses will carry us, but they refuse to carry the weight
of a grudge against their frustrating humans. Even horse relationships
are not severed when they are corrected or pushed around by another
horse. It's the way they're built.

Forgiveness is so easy for horses yet so difficult for us humans.

The truth is, people make mistakes not only with horses, but also
with each other. While forgiving someone can be difficult, holding a
grudge is worse. It doesn't make us stronger or better people. Instead, it

makes us bitter. I've heard it said that holding onto bitterness and unforgiveness is like eating rat poison and then waiting for the rat to die.

Forgiveness is not only about giving grace to others, but also about our own spiritual growth. Because God has forgiven all our sins, we should not withhold forgiveness from others: "Bear with each other and forgive one another if any of you has a grievance against someone. Forgive as the Lord forgave you" (Colossians 3:13).

If you have been carrying around the burden of a grudge, it's time to ask God to help you set things right. Take a lesson from your horse, and learn to forgive.

....

Lord, I praise You for forgiving me. Help me to do likewise and forgive others, amen.

14

TRUST THE DRIVER

And who knows but that you have come to your
royal position for such a time as this?
ESTHER 4:14

As a general rule, horses don't like trailers. Some of them don't want to go in, and some don't like coming out. I have horses that plant their feet at the trailer door. The trick is to walk them away and take another run at it. Sometimes you need to load their buddy first or bribe them with food.

Why are most horses not fond of trailers? They aren't sure where they are going or what awaits them when they get there. The ride doesn't make sense to the horse, although the driver knows where the horse is going.

Much like our horse friends, sometimes life makes us feel as if we're being pushed, pulled, and taken for a ride we don't always want to be on. But consider this: God has placed us where we are at this specific time for a reason. The assignment He has given us and the challenges we must endure don't always make sense. Sometimes we feel like giving up. Yet take heart and press on, for who knows? Like Queen Esther in today's scripture, you may have been planted in your specific job, church, family, or community "for such a time as this." Esther was able to save her people, the Jews, from annihilation because she had been chosen to be the wife of the king at a crucial time.

God wants to use you for His glory too. As a Christian, your life is not your own. It belongs to the One who created you, and He has a plan just for you. Trust the Driver, because He knows where you're going.

....

Lord, give me the strength to trust You more—even when life doesn't make sense. Give me the right attitude and the assurance that I am right where You want me, amen.

15

BLACK BEAUTY

God picked you out as his from the very start. Think of it: included in
God's original plan of salvation by the bond of faith in the living truth.
This is the life of the Spirit he invited you to through the Message we
delivered, in which you get in on the glory of our Master, Jesus Christ.
2 THESSALONIANS 2:14 THE MESSAGE

My favorite horses are the old ones, because I have found that giving them a nice place to live out their years has been very beneficial to my heart. Horses really like feeling safe, and I like mothering them. They keep my heart soft. I used to be guilty of keeping my heart hard to make it safe from pain or disappointment. And although a soft heart does feel more pain, it also feels more joy.

My love for older horses most likely began when I first read the story *Black Beauty*.

Throughout this wonderful tale, a character named Joe longs to find a horse, Black Beauty, from his past. At one point, he walks right past Beauty at a horse sale, and they fail to connect. But by the end of the adventure, Beauty finds his "savior" and lives the remainder of his life with Joe, who promises never to sell him.

There are many times in our lives when God reaches out to us, and we continue to miss our opportunities to connect with Him. For some of us, we may conclude we're just too old or too sin-ridden. We may feel as if

God couldn't love us, or that we'll never measure up to His standards. Or we may believe deep down that we are not worth saving. But understand this: God will never stop loving you. He will never stop desiring you to come to Him and be close to Him. Nothing you have ever done or will ever do will change that. If you doubt His love for you, study the stories in Scripture about His journey to the cross. He suffered every bit of that excruciating death for me and for *you*.

No matter your age, now is the time to live the remainder of your life with Someone who will always be with you and who will never sell you out. Accept God's invitation and get to know your Savior today.

....

Lord, I'm so glad that You picked me out as Your own—from the very start. You invited me to know You and live with You forever. I'll always be grateful for the home I have in You, amen.

16

ONE-EYED ROANIE

See what great love the Father has lavished on us,
that we should be called children of God!

1 JOHN 3:1

My best friend from childhood was a one-eyed quarter horse named Roanie. She was loyal and sweet. Roanie came to me when I was twelve years old and desperately needed a friend. When we went on rides together, she took care of me. We once got in a nest of bees, and she did not buck because I was on her back. She just took the pain.

At first glance, the world would see my broken horse as having little value. But if you were to ask me, her kind heart and gentle spirit made her *priceless* in my eyes. And that's how God views us too.

He sees us the way He has always seen us, as His precious children. Parents love their children with a depth of emotion and commitment that their kids will never understand (unless and until they have kids of their own). What's more, we love our children no matter how they act or what they do—good, bad, or ugly. Ponder this: God loves us even more than a mother loves her child. It's mind-blowing when you think about it.

Have you ever doubted your own worth? If so, remember how high God placed your value. Through the birth, life, death, and resurrection of His only Son, the Father paid the ultimate price to rescue us from our sin.

Don't let the things of this world determine your value. He has loved you since He knit you together in your mother's womb (Psalm 139:13), and He will love you for all eternity.

When the world makes you feel like that broken horse, remember this: *you* are priceless to God.

....

Lord, thank You for loving me just as I am. Thank You for declaring that I am a child of God—priceless in Your eyes, amen.

17

Follow the Trail Map

All Scripture is God-breathed and is useful for teaching, rebuking,
correcting and training in righteousness, so that the servant of
God may be thoroughly equipped for every good work.
2 Timothy 3:16–17

Your saddle creaks softly beneath you as your horse moves at a steady pace. With each step, your body loosens in sync with the rhythm of the trail ride—and you can't help but feel at peace with the world. It's just you and your horse in the wilderness. The sunshine melts away your stress, and the fresh, pine-scented air invigorates your senses. *Perfect.*

But suddenly you panic. *The map!* you think. *I forgot the trail map! What if we get lost? How will we find our way home? This is bad!*

As we navigate through life, it's so easy to get so busy being busy that we forget to prepare for the journey ahead. We get caught up in the details of everyday living—going to work, paying bills, taking care of others—and neglect the One who is able to make us wise, strong, and godly. We go our own way, forgetting to communicate with the fail-proof Source who knows what's around the bend and the exact route we should take.

God has provided us with the ultimate trail map to navigate us through life: the Bible. Dotting the pages of Scripture (like trail markers along the way) are promises to encourage us and warnings to keep us from danger. God knows the way because *He is the Way.*

Start reading the Bible today. There is no better time, and there's no reason to wait. When you follow the Lord's guidance, He will deliver you safely to your destination. And consider this: not only did God give us the map, *He created the trails!*

....

Lord, my life is often so busy that I set off on the journey without seeking You first. Help me to make Your Word a priority. Speak to me through Scripture so that I may be thoroughly equipped for every good work, amen.

18

JUST AS YOU ARE

You will again have compassion on us; you will tread our sins underfoot and hurl all our iniquities into the depths of the sea.

MICAH 7:19

One of my favorite things about horses and donkeys is that they couldn't care less about what you've done or where you've been. When one of my four-legged friends sees me, he neighs and calls out to tell me he loves me unconditionally. Isn't that what we love about our dogs too? They are always *so* glad to have us home. Animals love us without us having to do a thing. They accept us just as we are.

As much as our horses love us, that love pales in comparison to the incomprehensible love Jesus has for us. He loves us without reservation. He doesn't hold the past against us or wave it in front of us to make us feel guilty so we'll act right. Now, the enemy will do his best to hold the past over our heads, but as we come humbly before God, seeking forgiveness, He will cast our iniquities into the sea. God will take away our fear and our baggage. "How great is God's love for all who worship him? Greater than the distance between heaven and earth! How far has the LORD taken our sins from us? Farther than the distance from east to west" (Psalm 103:11–12 CEV).

We don't have to fix our weaknesses to be acceptable to God. He loves us just as we are. The best part is, He refuses to leave us in our sin with no way out. Through Christ, we can experience complete forgiveness.

So accept the unconditional love of the Father. He is waiting for you with open arms!

....

Lord, thank You for Your mercy and compassion. Thank You for pardoning my sin and loving me no matter what, amen.

19

THE EXTRAORDINARY ORDINARY

While walking by the Sea of Galilee, [Jesus] saw two brothers,
Simon (who is called Peter) and Andrew his brother, casting
a net into the sea, for they were fishermen. And he said to
them, "Follow me, and I will make you fishers of men."
MATTHEW 4:18–19 ESV

My horse has mended a broken heart a time or two. It's unfortunate that some people would say I own an "ordinary horse." He's never accomplished any of the things that would make him a champion in the eyes of others. But to me, he is an exceptional healer.

God has a habit of using what the world views as ordinary to perform His greatest miracles. Ordinary horses don't know they're ordinary, so why would we ever think we are? The Bible makes it clear that we are exceptional to God, designed with the purpose of doing exceptional things for His kingdom.

When Jesus called ordinary fishermen like Peter and Andrew to come and follow Him, He had a plan far beyond what they could imagine. I'm sure they never expected to be world-changers. Maybe they gravitated toward Jesus because they believed He was a prophet, or because He was magnetic. Perhaps they were simply sick of fishing. Who knows what was going through their minds?

However, in a few short years, God would use these two—and

others—to spread the gospel of Christ to thousands of people. Peter even became known as the rock on whom Jesus built the New Testament church.

Since God transformed the lives of "ordinary" fishermen and turned them into powerful and effective missionaries for His glory, imagine what He can do for *you*. Go forth with excitement, in His power, and get ready to be exceptional today.

....

Lord, thank You for making me anything but ordinary. I, too, want to be a fisher of men. Help me to go forth and do exceptional kingdom work, amen.

20

TRUE CONTENTMENT

*In any and all circumstances I have learned the secret of being
content—whether well fed or hungry, whether in abundance or in
need. I am able to do all things through Him who strengthens me.*
PHILIPPIANS 4:12–13 HCSB

My horse wraps his neck around my shoulders and nickers in my ear, *I love you.* This is how we speak to each other. Our bond is a gift that goes beyond me supplying his physical needs. My horse is content.

What would it take for you to be content? More money, more power, more status? These things are short-lived and ultimately leave us empty and dissatisfied. The Bible tells us that friendship with the things of this world results in hostility toward God (James 4:4). Scripture instructs us to keep our lives free from the love of money and to be content with what we have, because God has said, "Never will I leave you; never will I forsake you" (Hebrews 13:5).

True contentment is found in knowing God intimately and following His plan. It's not a place (or a station in life) we arrive at, but a choice we can make today.

The apostle Paul was content despite his challenging circumstances. While sharing the gospel, he was shipwrecked, beaten, tortured, and imprisoned. In fact, Paul wrote the book of Philippians from a jail cell.

How could he be content? Today's scripture shows he knew Jesus, and knowing His Savior was enough.

It's so easy to get caught up in envying people who have more resources than we have. If we're not careful, those feelings will build up like mold on hay. Remember: the things of this world are temporary and fleeting, but joy and contentment are eternal. Trust that God's peace is greater than the world's riches.

Lord, help me to be content in my walk with You. Show me how to be joyful "whether in abundance or in need," amen.

21

LOVED DISTINCTIVELY

God planned for us to do good things and to live as he has always
wanted us to live. That's why he sent Christ to make us what we are.
EPHESIANS 2:10 CEV

I am often asked which one of my horses is my favorite. To me, that question is the equivalent of asking me which one of my children I like better. After all, just like kids, every horse has his or her own special quirks. Some horses have ridiculous eating, sleeping, or bodily habits that keep us entertained for hours.

For instance, I have a couple of horses that pull their food out of the rack and onto the floor before they eat it. I once met a horse that would only eat green apples, not red ones, and I now own a pony named Cupcake who likes to suck on carrot pieces. Orlando likes to sleep in the same corner of his stall with his head over the automatic waterer, and Grandpa Spike is so old he falls asleep while drinking water.

When it comes to these four-legged friends, weird is wonderful.

God gave you the gift of uniqueness too—right down to your fingerprints, how you think, and your own special talents. God's gift set you apart from the rest of the herd. Do you love to sing? God has plans to use your voice somehow. Are you a book lover? He planned that too. Does your heart sing when you're enjoying the outdoors? He made you that way. Even those things that you think make you odd or different are part of you for a reason. God created you, and He thinks you're wonderful.

Now, don't worry about losing your individuality and becoming a clone when you commit your life to Christ. Our heavenly Father loves all His children equally—but also *distinctively.* God created you, made you with personal strengths and weaknesses, designed a unique plan for your life, listens to your personal prayers, and has unique ways of nurturing and maturing you. The fact that God loves us distinctively also helps us appreciate the uniqueness He has given to other believers.

Never forget: you are one of a kind. God loves *you.*

....

Lord, thank You for my uniqueness. Help me to use my gifts to do the things You planned for me to do, amen.

22

———◆———●————————●———◆———

HEMMED IN

*"Therefore I tell you, do not worry about your life, what you will
eat or drink; or about your body, what you will wear. . . . Can
any one of you by worrying add a single hour to your life?"*
MATTHEW 6:25, 27

One thing I love about horses is their lack of worry. I, however, worry too much. Case in point: I worry about falling off and breaking my neck. I'm actually allergic to horses (yes, I'm serious), so I worry about whether or not I packed my eye drops in my saddlebags. I even worry about where to take a bathroom break on the trail.

Maybe you've heard the old saying, "Don't put the cart before the horse." In other words, we worry about things before we have enough information about them. When we're faced with too little information and too much imagination, we can become our own worst enemy. Anxious thoughts swirl through our brains when we're tired, when we're sick, when we're inching our way through morning traffic, or when we're late for an important meeting. Fear kicks in as our safety is threatened and our circumstances slide out of control. Suddenly, our brains go on full alert, launching into a fight-or-flight state and sending adrenaline surging through our veins. (No need for that double-shot, supersized caffeine concoction!)

Did you know that more than 90 percent of the things we worry about never happen? The truth is, God is protecting us from ourselves. He has already gone before us and will guard us from behind: "You hem me in behind and before, and you lay your hand upon me. Such knowledge is too wonderful for me, too lofty for me to attain" (Psalm 139:5–6). Now that's something we can hitch our wagons to.

....

Lord, help me to give up worry. Give me the strength to be calm and to trust that You are in control, amen.

23

Our Trail Guide

Wait for the LORD; be strong and take heart and wait for the LORD.
PSALM 27:14

Horses want our leadership, and more than anything, they *need* it. Horses that are spoiled instead of benefitting from strong leadership end up frustrated and unhappy. As you may have experienced with your own horses, they often act up because of their insecurity. Those who are too impatient to stand still for mounting are potentially dangerous. At any moment, an unrestrained horse may decide to move in the opposite direction, leaving its rider face-first on the ground.

Spoiled, insecure, impatient. Sounds familiar, right?

If God didn't provide leadership and instead gave us everything we wanted the second we wanted it, our faith would be weak. Our focus would be inward, and the moment something didn't quite go our way, we'd conclude that the Lord had abandoned us. (Come to think of it, that isn't faith at all.)

We need the steadfast guidance of our heavenly Father. He is leading us along the trail, training us to impact the world for Him. Like our horses when we give them a gentle nudge with our heels, we need to move when God calls us to action. When He reins us to the side, we should be prepared to change course in our lives at His call. When He says, "Not yet," we need to stand patiently at the block and wait until the Lord tells

us it's safe to move forward. There is a potential danger for us if we move
n a direction without waiting on God.

Do you sense God's leading hand on your life? Are you finding it
hard to remain still before Him? Remember: He blesses those who wait
on Him, ultimately leading them exactly where they need to be.

....

Lord, I want Your will, not mine. Help me to trust Your leader-
ship and wait patiently for Your timing, amen.

24

THE NAP SCHEDULE

*Dear friends, don't forget that for the Lord one day is the same as a
thousand years, and a thousand years is the same as one day.*
2 PETER 3:8 CEV

You could set a clock to my horse Orlando's afternoon napping schedule. From two to four every afternoon, he's snoozing away in his
stall. Since Orlando is an old guy and enjoys his routine, I work around
his schedule and ride him only in the mornings. Otherwise, he's slow and
cranky as we ride.

Most of us enjoy feeling in control of our own schedules and grow
frustrated when things don't go according to plan. But just like my old
horse, we only *think* we are in control. Yet submitting to God's timetable
requires faith and courage. God has perfect timing: never too early, never
too late. He is never in a hurry, but He is always on time.

However, it can be difficult to rest in God's timetable. I don't know
about you, but I can be tempted to "help God out" and hurry Him along.
In the Old Testament, Sarah got impatient with God's delay in fulfilling His promise to give her and her husband, Abraham, a child. Instead
of waiting on God, she convinced Abraham to sleep with her servant,
Hagar. Unfortunately, the resulting baby caused more harm than good,
and the repercussions still echo today. God isn't a napper. He doesn't
take afternoons off from loving, protecting, and blessing us. He is patient

with us, giving us every opportunity to repent and to be saved. So ask God to help you be patient with His timing. Trust His ways, and don't waste a moment with the Lord.

....

Lord, I know You aren't slow about keeping Your promises. Teach me to be patient and wait on Your perfect schedule, amen.

25

FEAR OR FAITH?

Even though I walk through the darkest valley, I will fear no evil,
for you are with me; your rod and your staff, they comfort me.
PSALM 23:4

Horses are prey animals with a fight-or-flight instinct. At times, this characteristic can make a trail ride feel more like an adventure on a runaway train. I remember one ride when a combination of farm equipment and deer made my horse come unglued several times in quick succession. I tried to stay calm and cool, but I finally gave up and went home. When our horses spook, it can spook us too. And in those tense moments of fear, we're ready to cut our rides short.

This broken world can make us feel just as spooked. There are days when it's amazing that we even have the courage to leave our houses. But with God, we are given a choice between experiencing fear or faith. God wants so much more for us than to walk through life full of fear, worry, and anxiety. We may not be in control, but we can trust the One who is.

When fear strikes, the best thing we can do is kneel on those knocking knees. As we go to God in prayer, He gives us peace and comfort. He also provides answers to our prayers and performs miracles on our behalf. As we exercise these "trust muscles," they get stronger, and our faith begins to grow.

Try letting go of the reins and putting them into the capable hands of God. You still might spook on occasion, but the closer you get to the Lord, the more fear-proof you'll become.

....

Lord, drive fear out of my life. Help me to pray instead of worry. And as I pray, grow my faith, amen.

26

FOUR-LEGGED HEALERS

The LORD . . . heals the brokenhearted and binds up their wounds.
PSALM 147:2–3

God brings horses into our lives when He knows we need them most—whether we are lonely or deep in grief. In moments of vulnerability, horses encourage us and build us up. I have a horse named Rethel who helped a teenage girl mend a heart bruised by mean boys and bad friends. A pony named Charlie Brown helped another young person's heart heal from bullying. Orlando, one of my horses, took my mind off some health struggles.

But no matter how amazing horses are, the ultimate healing comes only from the Father.

God will bring the right scriptures, worship songs, and people into our lives when He knows we need them most. When we are lonely or in deep grief, He will send us His love in creative, diverse ways—through nature, an e-mail, or a movie scene. As we learn to trust Him to comfort us, we learn to go to His side more and more.

So when we feel injured and beaten down by circumstances, sin, and hurtful people, we can take our pain to God. He will mend our brokenness. In fact, Scripture tells us that the Lord will restore our joy: "You make known to me the path of life; you will fill me with joy in your presence, with eternal pleasures at your right hand" (Psalm 16:11).

Some things are beyond human repair and can only be restored by the loving-kindness of the Savior. Trust His healing work.

....

Lord, the Bible says You heal the brokenhearted and bind up their wounds. I need Your healing touch. Bring peace and joy to my heart, amen.

27

A LITTLE HELP AROUND THE BARN

*"But the Helper, the Holy Spirit, whom the Father will
send in my name, he will teach you all things and bring
to your remembrance all that I have said to you."*
JOHN 14:26 ESV

I t's nice to have help around the barn. Stable hands look after horses'
everyday needs and make sure they're healthy and in good condition.

We, too, have Someone to help us and encourage us to live our best.
The third person of the Trinity—the Holy Spirit—is our Guide, Helper,
Strengthener, and Advocate, sent by God to live in us and give us direction in every aspect of our daily lives. Jesus said, "If you love me, keep
my commands. And I will ask the Father, and he will give you another
advocate to help you and be with you forever" (John 14:15–16). Like the
Father and the Son, God the Holy Spirit is to be believed and obeyed.

Being filled with the Spirit results in an abundant and overflowing
life. Before I invited the Holy Spirit to work in my life, I felt like the world
around me was dull and gray. I had all the things that were *supposed* to
make me happy, but I found myself asking, "Is this my purpose? Is this
all there is?"

The Holy Spirit is God's divine intervention in my life. If we are willing to listen and obey, God uses the Holy Spirit in us to guide us to the
plan He has for our lives. I experience the blessings and lessons God has

for me as the Spirit opens and closes doors. It's a life of highs and lows but always in color.

If you're looking for a more full life, start walking in the Spirit today.

....

Lord, fill me with Your Holy Spirit and direct my steps. Help me to live my life in color, amen.

28

A JUICY TIDBIT

A gossip betrays a confidence; so avoid anyone who talks too much.
PROVERBS 20:19

Do you ever wonder what horses talk about as they gather around the hay bale? Perhaps they're discussing a juicy tidbit that's circulating around the barn.

If you've ever heard the latest gossip around the watercooler, you know it's tempting to join in. Because it's part of our sinful nature to build ourselves up by tearing others down, we need God's help to tame our tongues. God compared the tongue to poison (James 3:8) because He knows firsthand the damage it can do. In Psalm 141:3, David asked God to "set a guard over my mouth, LORD; keep watch over the door of my lips."

Gossip can ruin friendships, damage reputations, and break down our ability to trust others. It's always best to avoid someone who gossips. And if it is you who is struggling, ask God to help you bridle your tongue.

We never know how our influence for Christ will change the world. And just imagine how powerful our witness would be if we learned to tame our tongues. The Bible teaches the importance of using speech positively. Instead of passing on negative words, use words that will help heal the wounds of others. Proverbs is full of verses on this subject. Why not memorize a few of them to recite when you're tempted to gossip?

I'm convinced that if we are loving our neighbors as ourselves, we are loving like a horse does. And that means we are encouraging others and building them up, not gossiping or tearing them down.

....

Lord, guard my tongue. Teach me to use words that heal, not those that hurt. Help me to avoid gossip, amen.

29

THE ESCAPE ARTIST

*Do you not know that your bodies are temples of the Holy
Spirit, who is in you, whom you have received from God?*
1 CORINTHIANS 6:19

My Shetland pony, Tucker, can open almost any door with his lips.
Although it's extremely cute, this troublesome skill could lead
Tucker into a serious situation if I didn't put locks on the doors that lead
to potential danger. Just because Tucker *can* do something doesn't mean
he *should.*

That's true of us as well. Just because something is technically legal
for us to do doesn't mean it's spiritually appropriate. The Bible says that
our bodies are a gift from God—temples of the Holy Spirit—and we are
to use them to honor Him.

Think of the different actions you take each day with your body:
talking, eating, exercising (or not), drinking. Ask God to reveal His will
for you and then ask yourself, *Is everything I do in line with what God
wants for my life? Does it contribute to a life of holiness—or is it harmful to
my spiritual well-being?*

If you feel convicted that some part or parts of your day-to-day
choices are wrong, don't dwell in shame or guilt. Simply confess your
sin and ask the Father for help to do better. The truth is, no one is born

holy—and none of us can fake it by acting holy or thinking holy thoughts. We can't even pursue holiness unless God stirs that desire in our lives.

However, the more we seek God in all that we do, the more we will begin to think as He does and become the holy people He desires. We will become more inclined to choose to do the things that spiritually strengthen us. Our holiness comes by way of His cross. He breathes holiness into our lives, and He will present us as holy to the Father.

Lord, I know that my body is a temple of the Holy Spirit. I know that I am not my own; I was bought at a price. Empower me to honor You with my body. Teach me to be holy as You are holy, amen.

30

BEYOND OUR EXPECTATIONS

Now to him who is able to do immeasurably more than all
we ask or imagine, according to his power that is at work
within us, to him be glory in the church and in Christ Jesus
throughout all generations, for ever and ever! Amen.
EPHESIANS 3:20–21

J ust when we think God can't make horses any better, He goes a little further and gives us the therapy horse. If you have ever had the privilege of seeing these horses in action, you would know the care God takes when He knits each one of them together. Through the use of therapy horses, some children take their first steps, the nonverbal become verbal, and many people are enabled to go on to live amazing lives.

Some of the people who will experience life-changing results from therapy horses are reluctant to approach the animal at first. Gradually, these folks begin to understand and develop a relationship with the horses.

In the same way, some people are reluctant to approach God out of fear or misunderstanding of who He is. Often, these pre-believers become so bogged down with misguided ideas about what they think Christianity is that they miss out on having a relationship with God.

We have to step out of our comfort zones on occasion in order to learn something new—especially to discover how amazing God is. The great promise to those who seek the Lord is that He will be found. But we must take the time to seek the truth for ourselves: "You will seek me and find me when you seek me with all your heart" (Jeremiah 29:13).

God does not go beyond Himself, but He does go beyond our expectations. As He did on the cross and at Jesus' resurrection, He goes further than we could imagine and keeps on amazing us with His goodness.

....

Lord, I thank You for being there when I reached outside my comfort zone toward You. I praise You for going way beyond my expectations, amen.

31

AMPLIFY THE GOOD

Finally, brothers, whatever is true, whatever is honorable, whatever is just,
whatever is pure, whatever is lovely, whatever is commendable, if there is any
excellence, if there is anything worthy of praise, think about these things.
PHILIPPIANS 4:8 ESV

When feeding elderly and sickly horses, I have a product I like to use called Amplify. As its name says, it is a grain designed to amplify the amount of calories horses can consume. Extra calories help horses maintain a healthy weight, and Amplify is a great tool for horses needing the boost. However, this amplified calorie amount can work against horses if not used properly. Some horses can founder, or get laminitis of the foot, if they are given excess sugar and calories.

I think of our inner lives much like a horse that needs Amplify (stay with me and I'll explain). Our emotions can be used for good or bad, depending on how we feed them. The apostle Paul gave us a list of things to think about in today's scripture: things that are true, honorable, just, lovely, commendable, excellent, and praiseworthy. In light of this list, we can either dwell on positive things or allow our emotions to trip us up. It's up to us to give our thoughts and emotions good (positive, uplifting, godly) food.

If we fail to do this, we make bad decisions when we react to situations. When we feed on unholy thoughts or negativity, we are more likely to blow up or give in when the enemy tempts us to lose control. Suddenly, our negative emotions are on full display as we let them take over. Instead of letting our emotions lead the way, we need to pray and ask for help.

Life can be tough, but God is available to fortify us through the ups and downs. And emotions can be a blessing when we learn how to manage them.

Lord, help me to amplify the good things in my life and control my emotions, amen.

32

TOO GOOD TO BE TRUE

"And you will know the truth, and the truth will set you free."
JOHN 8:32 ESV

There is no such thing as a startle-proof horse. Although certain horses are more trustworthy than others, all horses are still prey animals. You can't guarantee a horse won't react to a situation with the fight-or-flight response God instilled in him. No matter what you are told about a horse, guarantees about behavior are too good to be true. Wherever and whenever you ride, you should always wear your helmet.

We Christians are sometimes told things that are too good to be true. Based on the size of some church congregations, a seeker or new believer may assume that everything the masses are being told is accurate. However, that's not always the case.

Some preachers sell the lie that a mixture of positive speech and thoughts, unwavering faith, and religious donations will improve your health and your bank account. According to these leaders, your new Christian life will be hunky-dory. Friends, the fantasy of a pain-free life is too good to be true. If these teachers decided to be truthful, their mission statements would read, "We can catch a fly with honey, and we catch even more with a pile of horse manure."

The fact is, bad things happen to godly people all the time. Our Savior never guaranteed us a pain-free life, and He loves us too much to promise that we won't have to endure trials. With each affliction, God shows us our emptiness and weaknesses, and He draws us closer to His grace. A flood brings flowers, a surgeon's scalpel brings healing, and a crucifixion brought salvation. Blessings can be bittersweet.

This world is guaranteed to buck you off and probably kick you around a little too. So put on your helmet. Tribulations wean us from this world and make us long for our home in heaven. Count it all joy. The best is yet to come.

Lord, help me tell the truth from lies. Give me Your endurance in the midst of suffering. Help me to count it all joy, amen.

33

A Big, Happy Neigh

*But encourage one another daily, as long as it is called "Today,"
so that none of you may be hardened by sin's deceitfulness.*
HEBREWS 3:13

Nothing is more encouraging than when my horse neighs to me from across the pasture. That big neigh is a happy noise that makes me feel like I'm his favorite person.

In contrast, I once met a gravelly, weathered horse trainer who always had a disparaging remark for people who hand-fed treats to their horses. He told those of us who dispensed kisses to our horses, "You're spoiling them." While I agreed that hand-feeding treats makes for pushy horses, there was no way I was going to feel pressured to stop puckering up for my pony. Then one day, when he thought no one was looking, I witnessed this same cowboy kissing his horse on the nose.

It's often said that our character is shown by how we treat people when no one else is looking. Like that weathered cowboy, why do we sometimes conceal our pleasant side and opt instead to show the ugly one? As a human, you might want to be unkind at times, but you don't have to act on it. Next time you feel tempted to show the world your mean streak, make a surprising change and do the opposite by saying something positive about or to someone.

When encouragement is absent from our lives, we feel unloved, unimportant, useless, and forgotten. A kind word (or a big neigh), however, can make our day. Encouragement is a simple and thoughtful gift, and it doesn't cost you a thing. If you're kind when everyone is looking, you will soon be known as a great encourager, and your example will help others do the same.

This world is filled with of plenty of "nay" sayers. Choose to be a "neigh" sayer instead, and let people around you know their value.

....

Lord, please give me an opportunity to encourage someone today. Allow my words to soften a hardened heart, amen.

34

LET GOD DRIVE

Offer the sacrifices of the righteous and trust in the LORD.
PSALM 4:5

Despite my husband being exceptional at pulling, navigating, and backing up a horse trailer, I find myself interjecting driving instructions to him during our trips together. The truth is, I'm inept at pulling a trailer myself, and I always need to ask him for his help. I can't do it for myself, but I have an opinion on how he can do it better. ("Hi, my name is Cara, and I am a backseat driver." *"Hi, Cara . . ."*)

This is true in my spiritual life as well. One of the hardest things for me to do is to submit to the will of God. I have an opinion about which path I think is best for me, and I am almost always operating out of fear.

Sometimes I find myself praying as if I'm trying to talk God out of the plans He has made. What I am really doing is backseat driving while attempting to trust God at the same time. I can't see what's up ahead, and I can't walk this road by myself, but I sure have an opinion on how God could do it better.

The best plan is made by the One who knows what is going on around the bend. If you want to experience the peace that comes with trusting God, let Him take the wheel. Instead of interjecting driving instructions along the tough parts of your trip, try gratitude instead, thanking Him for being your driver.

Lord, thank You for taking me to places so much better than I could have imagined. Forgive me for trying to take the steering wheel out of Your capable and loving hands, amen.

35

WAITING FOR THE SHOE TO DROP

Therefore do not worry about tomorrow, for tomorrow will worry about itself. Each day has enough trouble of its own.
MATTHEW 6:34

We put a lot of faith in our farriers, but as the day of our trail ride gets closer, some of us start to question whether our horses' shoes are solidly in place. Some people spend their whole ride missing the scenery because they are anxiously looking down, waiting for a shoe to drop.

What about you? When good things start to happen in your life, do you joyfully relish the moments and God's blessings? Or are you left with the sense that now something bad will have to happen in your life?

"Waiting for the other shoe to drop" is another way of saying "letting the enemy steal our joy." Waiting for something bad to happen in our lives can leave us feeling constantly anxious and living in fear. If you find yourself sabotaging relationships before people have a chance to hurt you, or if you are asking God to get your next big disappointment over with, then the enemy has a foothold in your life.

It is true, sometimes we lose a shoe, and sometimes we lose the whole horse. But by being afraid of the things that *could* happen, you are missing the joys that come in the in-between moments. Between major disappointments and major blessings, joyfully live your life. When negativity and fear start creeping in, take a tally of all the good things that happen to you in just one day.

Instead of waiting for the next shoe to drop, thank God for your shoes instead. When we focus on the negative, we are failing to notice that God is caring for us all the time. Embrace the journey and choose joy.

....

Lord, forgive me for worrying instead of enjoying Your bless-ings. Draw near to me and give me peace, amen.

36

OFFICER CHARCO

"Enter through the narrow gate. For wide is the gate and broad is the road that leads to destruction, and many enter through it. But small is the gate and narrow the road that leads to life, and only a few find it."

MATTHEW 7:13–14

My mini donkey, Officer Charco, will go through any open gate, no matter where it leads. It's a comical quirk that makes it very easy for me to lead him from one place to the next. (If my pastured horses were that eager to go through open gates, it would save me a lot of blood, sweat, and tears.)

Some people are like Officer Charco. They follow whatever teacher or author is "in," without considering if the leader in question has any real authority or integrity. These folks want to take the most popular route toward spiritual enlightenment instead of walking with Jesus along what the Bible calls the "narrow" road.

What about you? Are you easily led astray? Or are you determined to go Jesus' way, no matter the cost to your reputation or bottom line?

In today's world, we hear a lot about intolerance and narrow-mindedness. Often, those words are said in relation to Jesus-followers standing up for the truth. To the world, we may look foolish, but Jesus didn't take an opinion poll to determine the most popular way to our salvation. He simply told us, "I am the way" (John 14:6). He laid out a narrow path—the *only* way to God—with no alternate routes.

The narrow gate isn't hard to find; it's just not the popular choice. We humans often gravitate to what's most comfortable. Much like my horses, we'd rather enjoy a wide gate leading to temporary, green pastures than the narrow gate of self-sacrifice required to follow Jesus.

You might be mocked and ridiculed for pointing out the narrow way. However, if even one person finds Jesus because you cared enough to share Him, what others think of you shouldn't really matter. Jesus is the only way to God—and when He shuts the gate, it will be too late.

....

Lord, give me courage to choose Your way, no matter the cost.
And help me to lead others through the narrow gate, amen.

37

TRAINING IN TRUST

May God, who puts all things together, makes all
things whole . . . Now put you together.
HEBREWS 13:18–21 THE MESSAGE

A round pen is like a corral with no corners. One of my friends bonds with her horse Luke in a round pen because it limits the ways he can avoid the pressure of what she is asking him to do. Since it narrows the options available to Luke, he finds the right answer more quickly. Round-pen training gives my friend a foundation to build on.

When you're training a horse, ultimately, you're not just teaching him how to react (not panicking, being patient) or how to do a task (crossing a bridge or water). You're also teaching a horse to have enough confidence in you, the trainer, to do what you ask him to do. Only when there's complete trust between horse and rider do you find success.

Spiritually, God trains us too. He takes the skimpy faith of a new believer and gradually grows us into mature, seasoned Christians. Often, those training sessions involve painful situations and prayers that are not answered immediately. Think about it: almost every situation that produces fruit in us is one we'd rather not go through.

You may be doing the work of God and not seeing the progress you would like to see. Maybe you are finding it hard to accept that God has a purpose in your health struggles, or your petitions seem to fall on deaf ears.

When God teaches us patience through trials, it can feel as if we are running in circles in a round pen. However, God does not corral us to be cruel. He holds us in place to teach us to walk in His ways, not to stray, and to trust in Him.

When you want to scream, "I can't stand anymore!" remember that faith is easy to demonstrate when things are going our way, but our true tests of faith come through trials. God knows your limits and will reward you in the end. Stand firm. God has a plan for you, and it's a good one.

Lord, help me to trust You even when things aren't going my way. I want to grow in my faith so I can please You, amen.

38

EXPECT THE UNEXPECTED

My soul, wait silently for God alone, for my expectation is from Him.
PSALM 62:5 NKJV

It's disheartening: almost every other ad on "horses for sale" websites seems to advertise a "child-safe" or "husband-proof" horse. Many husbands only agree to ride because of their wives, so a husband-proof horse is one for people who don't usually ride or know much about horses. Rarely do these horses live up to the expectations that buyers put on them.

I wish people would do right by their horses and sell them with honesty. Sadly, when these falsely advertised horses fail us, the new owners recall the lies they read in the ad. If we have formed expectations about horses that they cannot live up to, it is not their fault.

Just as there are no perfect horses, there are no perfect churches or families. Faulty expectations can get us into a lot of trouble. When we expect perfection out of people or situations, it is not their fault. Rather, those dashed hopes are a product of our own flawed expectations.

The good news is, you have the power to change your expectations by simply changing your attitude. When obedience took the disciples to Jerusalem, they fully expected Jesus to be crowned their military king. Peter, James, John, and the other apostles believed Jesus would overtake the Romans by force, and when the Son of Man submitted to a sham trial and was nailed to a cross, they were devastated.

Because the Messiah failed to live up to what they had envisioned, the dispirited disciples missed the greatest victory of all time: the resurrection. Today, while God is still dashing the expectations of those who think they have it all figured out, He is also continually blessing the humble in ways they never saw coming.

Thankfully, Jesus turns His kingdom upside-down all the time by doing things differently than you or I would. God is mighty—and He's mighty unpredictable. So instead of slinking off in disappointment and turning tail when your expectations are not met, humbly make your way over to God. He will surprise you in glorious ways.

Lord, forgive me for expecting You to work in human ways. Give me eyes to see Your glorious plans, amen.

39

X-RAYING EVERYTHING

Satan himself masquerades as an angel of light. It is not surprising, then, if his servants also masquerade as servants of righteousness. Their end will be what their actions deserve.

2 CORINTHIANS 11:14–15

Lameness is a horse's most common ailment. It's often impossible to see what the problem is by looking at the outside of their hooves. While there are a multitude of ways horses can go lame, an X-ray can bring injuries to light. I've owned a few horses that needed X-rays. Most of them had something that required "stall rest," and they recovered fine. But one horse named Banner was diagnosed with navicular. It's an ailment that usually gets worse with time. With early detection, Banner was able to receive the treatment he needed. By X-raying a horse's feet, a vet can tell if the animal has something serious that needs to be dealt with right away. Exposing the issue brings forth a path to proper care and healing.

Sometimes we need spiritual X-rays to tell when Satan is trying to fool us. He will try to disguise himself as an "angel of light" and make it look as if he stands for something good. It takes discernment to expose the evil that needs to be dealt with.

I have learned to X-ray everything under the light of God's Word. When new jobs, relationships, or opportunities appear, I pray about them and seek the wisdom of Scripture. Today, we have so many great resources—online Bible study tools, church Bible study groups, concordances, dictionaries, and historical texts—to assist us in our quest for God's truth. Some seminaries are now offering free Bible courses online that are open to anyone with a computer and Internet access. Why not purchase a study Bible and read a bit of it daily? Start with Psalms or the gospel of John if you feel overwhelmed.

Don't let Satan get you off track. When you know more of the Bible, the Holy Spirit will remind you of key verses as you go about your daily routine. If you're willing to put in the work, God's Word will expose the truth and keep you spiritually strong.

....

Lord, teach me to be discerning and not to let the enemy fool me. Keep me planted squarely in Your truth, amen.

40

The Source of Joy

*The minute I said, "I'm slipping, I'm falling," your
love, GOD, took hold and held me fast.*
PSALM 94:18 THE MESSAGE

Have you ever been on a saddle that was slipping because the girth strap wasn't tight enough? You try to keep your balance by shifting to one side or the other, but if you're not careful, you'll go over the side and end up on the ground.

God's love is like that girth strap. Without it, we find life is off-kilter. Before I knew the Lord, it looked from the outside as if I had everything a woman could want. I had a successful career, great friends, a fun job, nice things—but something was missing. I tried first one thing and then another, searching for the one philosophy or belief system that would finally fulfill me.

Still, from the first time I started considering the possibility that God was real, it took me twenty years to believe in the healing power of Jesus Christ. As it turns out, instead of me seeking God, God was pursuing me the whole time.

Don't let anyone tell you that God doesn't care about the little details of your life. God is concerned about *everything* that happens to us. No worry is too big or too small for His attention. When we give God our problems, He promises to give us the peace that transcends all understanding. What God wants most is a relationship with *you*. Find your balance and your identity in Him, and He'll hold you tight.

....

Lord, when I feel as if I'm slipping, I need Your love to hold me fast, amen.

41

Rx for a Doubt-Riddled Faith

*And without faith it is impossible to please God, because
anyone who comes to him must believe that he exists and
that he rewards those who earnestly seek him.*

Hebrews 11:6

Sometimes the bond between horse and owner needs to build over time. My best relationships with horses are the ones that didn't come easily. Just when I would have my doubts about whether we were going to work out, I would get a response from my horse that would draw us closer together. I once owned a Fjord horse named Gus. When he first came to my farm, Gus was very naughty. I thought I made a huge mistake by getting him. But over time, we learned to trust each other, and we started to have small breakthroughs. Eventually, he figured out I was worth trusting and that I would keep him safe.

I'd venture to say that almost all of us struggle with trusting God occasionally. The remedy for that is faith, and faith comes by studying the Word of God and being in His presence day in and day out.

I study and spend time with God in a variety of ways. I enjoy listening to a lot of sermons. My favorite preachers are Dr. David Jeremiah and Greg Laurie (I love evangelism, and I believe God has called me to it.) Talking to others about what Jesus Christ has done in my life and what He can do in theirs helps build my faith. I also speak to God to seek what

He wants me to do to glorify Him. I read the Bible and do Bible studies (right now I am doing a study on Jonah). I attend church on Sundays and use Bible apps.

When you draw near to God in worship, over time He will draw near to you in response. A close relationship to God doesn't come easily, but trust me. It will be worth it.

....

Lord, strengthen my faith and help me when I don't trust You completely. I praise You for being my Lord and Savior, amen.

42

You Can't Fool a Horse

Nothing in all creation is hidden from God's sight. Everything is uncovered and laid bare before the eyes of him to whom we must give account.
Hebrews 4:13

Horses rely on the energy around them to help them navigate life. When we are feeling burdened, they sense our low energy and feel how we are feeling. You cannot fool a horse. They are great judges of character and moods.

We can't fool God either. It's impossible to try to get anything past Him. In the garden of Eden, Adam and Eve naively attempted to hide from God after they disobeyed His commands. God knew exactly what they'd been up to, of course, and He knew where they were, but He still called out, "Where are you?" and came looking for them.

That story is good news for us. Even when we've messed up, God doesn't stop pursuing us. He seeks us out in our messes and mistakes because He loves us unconditionally.

Why do we try to hide from God? He already knows where we are and what we've done. He knows our moods and our doubts, our struggles and our burdens. He knows our character and what we're capable of, both the good and the bad.

Just as He pursued Adam and Eve, He's looking for you and longing for your presence. He's more than ready to hear you and forgive you.

When you are burdened with sin, confess it to God. True repentance will always result in God's mercy and forgiveness.

....

Lord, forgive me for hiding from You when I sin. I praise You for Your mercy. Hear my confession and cleanse my heart, amen.

43

ONE IN CHRIST

There is neither Jew nor Gentile, neither slave nor free, nor is there male and female, for you are all one in Christ Jesus.
GALATIANS 3:28

M are or gelding, buckskin or black, Shetland or Arabian? The huge variety of horses is as vast as the number of differing opinions about which breed or color is best. Thankfully, horses are not opinionated when it comes to the outside appearance of people. Horses will diligently carry us, no matter our race, gender, or social status. We are each truly equal in their eyes.

Every believer has equal standing in God's eyes too. In the early church, many different ethnic groups worshiped together for the first time. Understandably, the mixing of people who were used to being separate caused a lot of issues. In his letters to the believers in Galatia, Paul had to make it clear to them that they were all in the gospel-preaching business together. No longer would Jews and Gentiles be separated; rather, they would learn the same stories and share the same cup and wine. I'm sure some of the Jesus believers were scandalized by the freedom Paul preached. They simply weren't used to the radical nature of grace.

Today, we still tend to separate ourselves into factions. Think about your faith community. Do homeschooling families look down on public schoolers? Do stay-at-home moms from your church disparage the working-away-from-home moms? Maybe you've been guilty of judging another believer's piety by his or her media choices or Facebook posts.

When we look down on a person created in God's image, we are hurting somebody God loves and for whom Jesus died. God does not show partiality or favoritism, and neither should we.

....

Lord, thank You that I am in equal standing with others in Your eyes. Thank You that all believers are one in Jesus Christ, amen.

44

The Founder of Fun

"Blessed are the pure in heart, for they will see God."
MATTHEW 5:8

W hen I was about fourteen years old, I had to put down my horse Roanie after she received a brain cancer diagnosis. The loss of my friend made me so sad that I vowed never to grow close to another horse again. It wasn't until many years later that I considered the possibility of owning another horse. When the barn my daughter was riding at offered one of their horses to me for sale, I realized I was missing out on life by guarding my heart. I then purchased my horse Orlando.

When I softened my heart to the idea that it wasn't too late for me to ride, it opened up my life to so many new experiences and friendships. A soft heart feels more pain—but it also experiences more life.

God's Word is clear that the condition of your heart is critical in your walk with the Lord. Fifteen years ago, any Christian crossing my path would have considered my heart hard and untouchable. But one day, the words Jesus said on the cross, "Father, forgive them, for they do not know what they are doing" (Luke 23:34), softened my heart enough to let it hear the truth that I, too, could be forgiven.

We all have people in our lives who may be trying to run far from God. Although it seems like a waste of time to continue praying for unbelievers and hardened hearts, that's when we should pray harder. After

Jesus prayed for His enemies that day on the cross, a hardened criminal found forgiveness and a Roman centurion acknowledged Jesus as the Son of God.

Pray for unbelievers to open their hearts. And pray for your heart to remain soft to the Holy Spirit and all the joys God wants to give you.

....

Lord, help me to keep a soft heart toward You and all You want to give me, amen.

45

LIVE FREE

It is for freedom that Christ has set us free. Stand firm, then, and do not let yourselves be burdened again by a yoke of slavery.
GALATIANS 5:1

The idea of horses living free in the wild is an alluring thought, indeed. But the truth is, all wild horses need human help to survive. Drought, starvation, and roaring mountain lions are just some of the worries "free" horses have that our barn horses do not. In other words—an existence full of worry, fear, and death is not a way to live free at all.

Being a non-follower of Christ may be presented by some non-believers as a liberating existence. But living outside God's Word—and paying the consequences of sin—is anything but freedom. It's slavery.

Think of a man who does whatever he pleases, no matter the fallout. He works hard for his money so he buys a lot of stuff. On the weekend, he drinks too much, which leads him to get addicted to alcohol. After some time, he gets fired from his job because he can't be counted on. He loses his home because he can't make the payments without a job. He ends up lonely, depressed, sick, and broke. Or picture a woman who decides she doesn't need a traditional marriage to be happy. She goes from man to man, using them to get her physical and emotional needs met. But after a few years of her swinging lifestyle, she looks around at friends with children and families and starts to question whether she made the right choices. Now she has no deep relationship with a man. And she can't have children because she has mistreated her body so badly.

Does that sound liberating? Not at all. The truth is, God gave us the Bible and commands us to obey the words in it in order to protect us. He knows us better than we know ourselves, and He wants to give us what we truly long for: unconditional love, purpose, and meaning.

True liberation comes from knowing Christ and abiding in His Word. Trust Him to guide you in ways that are best for you. Live free.

....

Lord, I praise You for the freedom from sin and death You give to everyone who commits his or her life to You. Help me never again to be burdened by a yoke of slavery, amen.

46

FOALS WITH POTENTIAL

Sitting down, Jesus called the Twelve and said, "Anyone who wants to be first must be the very last, and the servant of all."

MARK 9:35

Every foal born on my farm has so much potential. Of course, my dreams for them are always much bigger than reality. In my heart, they are all World Cup winners, and that includes my donkeys.

Every child born on this planet has dreams—dreams that can be much bigger than how their lives ultimately turn out. Ask any child what she wants to be when she grows up, and the possibilities are endless. From becoming the president of the United States to the scientist who cures cancer, there is always such potential. However, there are few who pick "service" as a dream job.

Because we serve such a mighty God, we make the mistake of thinking everything He wants us to do for Him must be done on a huge scale. That's not always the case, especially when our calling is less than glamorous. But God puts us in places where we will be most effective for His glory, and that could mean working the counter at your local gas station.

Charles Spurgeon never went to college or seminary, and his first lessons in theology were from a lunch lady. Thanks to this perfectly placed, servant-hearted woman, the Prince of Preachers grew up to change the world. Who might you influence at your place of service?

Are you ashamed because you are "only a _____"? What would God say? With His eternal mind-set, He sees unlimited potential in each of us to influence people for Christ right where we are. You might never know (this side of heaven) the impact you have made. After all, our reality doesn't begin and end on earth. And God's plans are much bigger and better than we can imagine.

Lord, make me a servant. Let my faithfulness be an instrument of the gospel, wherever You place me, amen.

47

BIT VERSUS BIT-LESS

Make every effort to keep the unity of the Spirit through the bond of peace.
EPHESIANS 4:3

As much as I enjoy horses, there have been a few that I've had a hard time loving. If I were to judge all horses by the few I didn't connect with, I would be missing out on the joyful bonds I have with the ones I do. People, like horses, come in all types, and some of them are harder to love than others. And divisive issues bring out the difficult-to-love parts of all of us.

One place this truth is on display, for instance, is in a debate you find in the horse world. There are many bit-and-bridle types and variations, each made to apply pressure to a horse in a specific manner. I do not consider myself horse savvy enough to offer an educated opinion to the bit-versus-bit-less debate. But ask anyone who is a member of a social media group involving horses, and they will tell you: the strong opinions held on the subject often lead to name-calling and furious anger.

Why are we so hard to get along with at times? What makes us so self-righteous about things like horse bits? When we get frustrated by the things we can't control, we have the potential to lose control ourselves. It's easy to recognize people around us who want to control us and other people. It's harder to recognize controlling behaviors in ourselves.

Every time we surf the Internet or step outside our homes, we have the potential of dealing with difficult people (and becoming difficult people ourselves). We can't change a person or how that person chooses to live his or her life. Trying to control people is like trying to bridle the wind. But we can choose our own behaviors and what boundaries we need to set in our relationships. We can also pray to see people as God sees them.

This world is full of all types of human beings. Don't let a few difficult folks rob you of the joy of healthy relationships with lovely people.

....

Lord, enable me to see people as You do. Give me patience around difficult people, amen.

48

"Hello"

"This, then, is how you should pray."
MATTHEW 6:9

Most of us won't remember the first conversation we had with our horses, but it had to have started with some form of "Hello." I like to say hello with a brush. Brushing horses builds trust between both human and horse. Brushing makes the horse—and you—calm. It's my favorite language to use with horses as we grow closer.

One of the best ways to grow closer to God is to speak to Him in prayer. It doesn't have to be complicated or fancy. Prayer is a conversation with God.

However, feeling as if you don't know what to say or how to say it is common for new believers (and even faithful people who've believed for a long time).

The disciples admired the miracles Jesus did and the comfortable, direct way He talked with God. So they asked Him to teach them to pray. That's why Jesus gave us the Lord's Prayer. It's an excellent outline for prayer.

The prayer begins with praise: "Hallowed be your name" (Matthew 6:9). Beginning our prayers with praise gets us in the right frame of mind. Next, Jesus humbly surrendered to God and agreed with His plan and purposes: "Your kingdom come, your will be done" (v. 10). The prayer continues with a request for provision and mercy: "Give us today our daily bread. And forgive us our debts" (v. 11–12). It ends by asking God to guide and protect His children.

There is nothing wrong with reading and saying a prayer written by others; just make sure whatever you say, it comes from your heart.

God is listening. He longs for a relationship with you. So don't delay. Start the conversation by simply saying, "Hello."

Lord, thank You for examples of powerful and effective prayer. Teach me to pray, amen.

49

REAL TRAILERING

Because of the LORD's faithful love we do not perish, for His mercies never end. They are new every morning; great is Your faithfulness!
LAMENTATIONS 3:22–23 HCSB

I would confidently pull a horse trailer all day long if the road I traveled was guaranteed to be straight and hazard-free. But real trailering involves lots of backing up, sudden stops, and winding roads.

Committing to a Christian life doesn't guarantee straight paths either. Because we live in a fallen world, each of us can be sure to encounter potentially compromising situations, sudden interruptions, and other speed bumps that can slow us down or trip us up. Even after committing to Christ, we are still sinners who aren't free from sin's temptations. Becoming a Christian doesn't make you perfect; it just makes you saved. Thankfully, God has promised never to let you be tempted beyond what you can bear (1 Corinthians 10:13). He will provide a way out so you don't have to sin.

Your journey in Christ most certainly will not be a straight line. Rather, it will involve hazards and detours. You'll be forced at times to back up, recalibrate, and learn from your mistakes. Yet, if you mess up royally and break one of His laws, He promises to forgive you if you confess with a contrite spirit.

I don't know about you, but I'm glad God is with me on life's road trip. Through all the twists and turns, we can be sure that above all else God surrounds us with His faithful love.

Lord, thank You for Your faithfulness. Thank You for not letting me be tempted beyond what I can bear, amen.

50

Never Alone

"And surely I am with you always, to the very end of the age."
MATTHEW 28:20

Horses desire companionship—and they also require it. Relying on each other helps horses feel safe. As prey animals, they are wired to want an extra set of eyes to help watch for predators. You may have noticed that lone horses are often depressed.

Just as horses need companionship, so do people. We all need someone to talk to, but sometimes we feel isolated. Sometimes we feel lonely even when we are not by ourselves. There's a big lie the enemy wants you to believe: you are all alone. All of us, at least once in our lives, have allowed this lie to take up residence in our minds. Satan's goal is to isolate us, set us aside, and make us feel unimportant. He wants us to view our problems as evidence that God has abandoned us or that we are unlovable.

However, we don't have to play the deceiver's game. Let your feelings promote a positive change. Instead of running from your loneliness or denying it's real, use it to let God in. Remind yourself of the truth that God is with you and for you. Before He ascended to heaven after His resurrection, Jesus said, "I am with you always." He did not say "sometimes" or "only on Sundays." He said *always*, and He meant it. While all the other religions say, "Do such and such, and maybe you can be more spiritual," Christianity says God is already with us.

You are not alone in this life, so don't choose to go at it alone. By inviting Jesus into your heart, you are gaining a friend who is closer than a brother and wants to reveal the purpose He has for you. God has a plan for your life, and it's a good one. Let God fill up your empty places by accepting His love today.

Lord, I sometimes feel lonely, but I thank You that You never leave me. Teach me to claim the truth of Your presence whenever I feel alone, amen.

51

SHAKEN UP

*"For I know the plans I have for you," declares the LORD, "plans to
prosper you and not to harm you, plans to give you hope and a future."*
JEREMIAH 29:11

It's rare, but occasionally my horse Sven gets loose. The perfect combination of tall, green grass and compromised fencing is just too great a temptation for him to pass up. Even though Sven thinks he's happier grazing in the ditch by the road, it's a dangerous place. So I shake a bucket of grain to gain his attention so he will follow me back to the safety of the barn.

Like me with that bucket of grain, God likes to shake up our lives to get our attention when we succumb to the false sense of happiness that this world provides. A while back, I had a great job and husband and two healthy kids. We were financially secure. So where was God going to shake things up? With my health. Not only did it shake me up, but it proved to me that God also has a sense of humor.

I had planted an orchard of fruit trees on my property—and I became intolerant of fruit sugar. God even took away my ability to drink *coffee*! By taking away the one thing I really had no control over, my health, God got my attention. It was in those moments that I moved from being a Jesus believer to a Jesus *follower*. I began actually having a relationship with my Creator. I wasn't in control of any of it, and I finally realized I didn't want to be.

You know what I discovered? Even when He gives us a way out of the ditch, we get angry at Him for not wanting us to be happy. But God isn't trying to torment or sabotage us. A loving Father, God shakes the bucket to protect His children, not to antagonize them. He wants to lead us back to the specific path He has for each of us.

....

Lord, shake up my life and do whatever is necessary to keep me on the path to eternal life. I know that lasting happiness can only be found in a deeper relationship with You, amen.

52

THE GOOD NEWS

Give praise to the LORD, proclaim his name; make
known among the nations what he has done.
PSALM 105:1

Despite the benefits that come from dealing with horses, I have had those occasional moments when I had to deal with bad news. Horse injuries, debilitating illnesses, and loss of life are unfortunate life lessons that come with owning horses.

The only benefit of bad news is that we can't appreciate the good news without it.

As Christians, we hear a lot about the good news but not enough about the bad. The unfortunate thing is that we can't have the good news without it. The bad news is that we are all sinners. If we say we have no sin, we deceive ourselves. But if we understand that we are destined for hell because of our sin, we can appreciate all that Jesus did for us on the cross.

Our loving Lord took on Himself the penalty for our sin. Every day, we choose to disobey the commands God has given us. If God were not merciful, we would die in our sin and be separated from Him forever. However, God longs for a restored relationship with us, and He wants to spend eternity with us. That's why He sent Jesus to live a sinless life and take our punishment by surrendering to a gruesome death. He died in our place so that we don't have to suffer judgment.

Once you recognize that you are a sinner, you can accept a Savior. Then the bad news turns to good, and you can't help sharing the gospel (literally, "good news") with others.

Heaven is not for good people; heaven is for forgiven people.

Lord, thank You for being faithful and just and for forgiving my sins. Empower me to share the good news with people I encounter every day, amen.

53

BARN CHORES

"Father, if you are willing, take this cup from me;
yet not my will, but yours be done."
LUKE 22:42

A funny horse meme circulates around social media every winter. It's a picture of a frozen Jack Nicholson from the movie *The Shining*. The caption reads, "Horses are fed, but I can't feel my face or fingers anymore."

On days when the weather is harsh and unmerciful, this meme makes light of the things we have to get done. As humans, it is in our nature to try to get the biggest result with the least amount of effort. If there were any possible way to get our barn chores done from the warmth of our homes, we would choose this path. But because we love our horses and there is no other possible way, we buck up, gear up, and do our chores to the best of our ability.

In the Garden of Gethsemane, Jesus prayed to His Father three times, saying, "My Father . . . take this cup from me." Jesus was fully God, but He was also fully human in every way. His human nature was perfect, but He was still battling to accept the torture and the shame He knew awaited Him. In other words, He was asking His Father if there were any other way.

Out of His love for us and His obedience to God, He willingly laid down His life when He voluntarily went to the cross to die for us. Jesus took the hardest way possible to narrow our road down to two possible choices: We can either receive Him into our lives or decide to live apart from God.

Jesus gives us hope against the sting of every sin when we invite Him into our hearts. He is the only way to break the bindings of this harsh and unmerciful world.

Make it a priority to receive Him into your life today and share Him with others.

Lord, forgive me for sometimes choosing the easy path over the best path. Thank You for Jesus, who sets the example for me, amen.

54

THE PONY EXPRESS

He said to them, "Go into all the world and preach the gospel to all creation."
MARK 16:15

In the mid-1800s, three creative men brainstormed and implemented a plan to allow mail to reach long distances quickly—by riders traveling on horseback. According to HistoryNet, "The lack of speedy communication between the mid-west and the west was accentuated by the looming threat of a civil war. Russell, Waddell and Majors designed a system that spanned . . . over one hundred stations, each approximately two hundred forty miles [apart], across the country."[2]

The Pony Express, as it would come to be known, consisted of four hundred to five hundred horses and about eighty deliverymen. The riders traveled a route from the Midwest to California. In spite of operating for only nineteen months, the Pony Express horse-and-rider relay teams successfully traveled more than 500,000 miles and delivered some 35,000 pieces of mail across the American frontier. Amazingly, though the job was hard and perilous, all but one delivery made it to its destination. If that sounds impressive, consider the job the disciples had to spread the Word of Christ across the whole known world. There weren't many people to carry this news, and they faced hostility everywhere they went. But unless brave disciples delivered the gospel to the lost, the message couldn't get out.

Jesus calls us to preach the gospel too—but some of us think we're not strong enough or smart enough to handle this task. Just remember that God doesn't call the qualified but qualifies those He calls.

Start with your family and then work your way across God's frontier. The good news is only good news if it gets there on time.

Lord, empower me to share the good news with those around me: my family, my neighbors, my coworkers. Give me the words to share and the confidence to share them, amen.

55

YOUR LONGEST TRAIL RIDE

Brothers and sisters, I do not consider myself yet to have taken hold of it. But one thing I do: Forgetting what is behind and straining toward what is ahead, I press on toward the goal to win the prize for which God has called me heavenward in Christ Jesus.

PHILIPPIANS 3:13–14

Your commitment to your Christian faith is without a doubt your longest trail ride. One sure way to get burrs of discouragement under your saddle is to start comparing your ride to someone else's who has been doing it longer. The truth is, even the person whom you most admire as a Christian leader is still in need of spiritual growth. He or she is not perfect, just as you aren't perfect—until you're in heaven.

The transformation God does in our lives through Christianity—growing us in the likeness of Christ—is not accomplished overnight. Rather, it's a lifelong process.

Don't focus too much on the rides of others, and don't look back at the mistakes you have made along the way. Satan loves to get believers off track by sowing seeds of discontent, jealousy, and discord. He also likes to plant half-truths and demonic lies, such as, "You'll never amount to anything. Just look at your past!" or, "You'll never be as good a Christian as her. Why keep trying?"

In his letter to the Philippians, Paul urged them to keep their eyes on the prize: the crown of glory awaiting them in heaven. It's an inspirational and oh-so-practical book. Paul encouraged the early church (and us) not to get distracted by worldly concerns, past mistakes, or the actions of others.

Plant your feet in the Bible daily, and learn scriptures to defend yourself against the devil's attacks. As you replace the enemy's lies with God's truth, you will grow in maturity and feel more peace and joy.

With your Bible as your compass, move toward what is ahead. Forward is heavenward.

....

Lord, give me the strength to deepen my Christian walk—to press on toward the goal. I want to win the prize: eternity with You, amen.

56

YEARNING FOR HOME

Then Jesus told him, "Because you have seen me, you have believed;
blessed are those who have not seen and yet have believed."
JOHN 20:29

I once purchased a horse from someone who felt she no longer had time to care for him. Despite my showering this horse with hours of affection, lush pastures, and horse companionship, he never seemed to accept my farm as his home. Eventually, I called his previous owner who was more than eager to take him back. This horse had once found his true home, and he yearned to return to it.

Like that horse, believers are offered all kinds of things by this world, yet, we still yearn for something we can't see. Faith is believing in God and His promises without ever seeing Him. Because we can't actually lay eyes on God, our faith can falter at times. That's why God provides times of trial and testing: to prove that our faith is real and to sharpen and strengthen it. When we stay in God's Word by reading the Bible, we witness the importance of faith. (If you want to read about some inspiring, faithful heroes in Scripture, take some time to read through Hebrews 11, which some scholars call the Hall of Faith.)

What does "walking in faith" mean? It means knowing that when I do the wrong thing, I am forgiven. It means believing that God really knows what is best for me, and trusting that He has my best interests at heart, even when things don't make sense to me. To live by faith means to have trust in God even when our days get difficult. It's how we persevere.

When it comes to Christian faith, you must believe to see.

....

Lord, I long to have faith, even when I can't see. Please strengthen my faith, amen.

57

"Gospel Traders"

"Watch out for false prophets. They come to you in sheep's clothing, but inwardly they are ferocious wolves. By their fruit you will recognize them."
MATTHEW 7:15–16

H orse traders use half-truths to sell horses for personal gain. But these small lies can return big consequences, both for the misrepresented horse and the safety of the buyer. Partial truth still isn't truth, and it's a common tactic of the enemy.

Unfortunately, there are plenty of false teachers telling half-truths about the gospel. They mix enough accurate biblical information in with their lies so that they seem to be preaching the truth. Whether they are doing it for wealth or to pack the pews, their feel-good messages and books give believers a false sense of security by preaching all flowers and sunshine. These ear-ticklers proclaim a false god who wants us all to be happy, wealthy, and successful. Now, God *is* full of grace and mercy, but He also expects us to turn from our sins once we accept the gospel.

Too many people have been lured away from orthodoxy by these lie-peddlers. Then, when jobs, relationships, or the health of people they love go south, they are either convinced that they are full of sin, that they lack faith, or that God is punishing them, or they resolve that God is not a good or real God after all.

God does not promise that He'll make you rich, keep you healthy, or free you from life's storms. But He does promise to carry you through all situations.

To avoid these "gospel traders" you need to search the truth out for yourself. Study the Bible, pray for guidance from the Holy Spirit, and you will recognize these people by their fruit.

....

Lord, help me to discern who is teaching falsehoods and grant me wisdom to know which teachers and pastors I can trust, amen.

58

BRINGING OUT THE BEST IN US

*Unlike the culture around you, always dragging you
down to its level of immaturity, God brings the best out
of you, develops well-formed maturity in you.*
ROMANS 12:2 THE MESSAGE

Show me your horse, and I'll tell you who you are.

These special friends mirror us, exposing our true selves—warts and all. They sense when we're happy or sad, at peace and in pain. They nuzzle their way into our hearts and help us work through our hang-ups. And as they help us see our true selves, they bring out the best in us.

If we let Him, God will bring out the best in us.

He, too, understands us and senses our pain and joy. He helps us work through our hang-ups and see our true selves—warts and all. Then, if we're willing to surrender to Him, He molds us and makes us into the best version of ourselves, the selves He saw when He formed us. It's not an easy path, this walk of faith. But it's so worth it.

Our transformation begins with a crucial first step. If we're to become more like Jesus—and the best "us" we can be—we must understand that life challenges don't *make* us who we are; they *reveal* who we are. We can take what is revealed through our challenges and use that as an opportunity to point us in a new direction. And if we trust in God, the challenge will strengthen our faith.

Here's a truth we would do well to plant deep in our hearts: "Consider it pure joy, my brothers and sisters, whenever you face trials of many kinds, because you know that the testing of your faith produces perseverance. Let perseverance finish its work so that you may be mature and complete, not lacking anything" (James 1:2–4).

The hotter the fire, the purer the gold.

....

Lord, help me to see problems as opportunities to become more like Jesus. Bring out the best in me, amen.

59

GETTING BACK ON THE HORSE

*"Do not fear, for I am with you, do not be afraid, for I
am your God; I will strengthen you, I will help you, I
will uphold you with my victorious right hand."*
ISAIAH 41:10 NRSV

Riding horses can be a dangerous activity, and I will admit that I struggle with bouts of fear that seem to come just before a big trail ride. Horses are big animals, and you never can tell what is going to spook one. We've all heard the saying, "If you fall off a horse, you have to get right back on." Even for seasoned riders, this can be difficult.

I experience this in my everyday world too. Despite giving my life to Jesus Christ and engaging in His Word daily, I am still not able to completely overcome occasional fear. The truth is, fear can paralyze our faith, and it gives the enemy an opportunity to steal our peace. During those moments when fear is churning in our hearts, there is only one thing we should do: talk to God. In Jesus' name, we can (and should) tell the enemy to hit the bricks. The devil will do his best to get us off track, but he will lose his foothold when we determine to trust God more than what we fear.

It strikes me that our Christian walk could be described as "falling off and getting right back on." We fall off in fear or sin; we get back on with prayer and confession.

Our spiritual growth is an ongoing process that is not for the faint of heart. But with determination to get back in the saddle after we fall away, we will ultimately get to ride off to the freedom that only God can provide.

Remember: God is bigger, so fear not.

....

Lord, sometimes fear grips my heart, and it's almost more than I can bear. During those moments, help me to turn to You. Give me courage and restore peace in my life, amen.

60

Embracing the Lifestyle

*You're going to find that there will be times when people will have no stomach
for solid teaching, but will fill up on spiritual junk food—catchy opinions
that tickle their fancy. They'll turn their backs on truth and chase mirages.*
2 Timothy 4:3–4 The Message

Horse ownership means that we are making a commitment to a horse—*and* that we are willing to accept the lifestyle change that comes with it. Nothing says unconditional love like leaving your warm house to feed horses when it's fifteen degrees below zero outside. Once we commit to ownership, even in trying times, there are many joys and benefits that come with it.

Some people want the love and forgiveness of Jesus Christ but not the accompanying lifestyle change. Yet we must ask ourselves if we're on a *truth quest* or a *happiness quest*. We can always find a person, web page, or even a church that will promote lies—spiritual junk food—that sound good but lack the whole truth of the Bible.

When it comes to a horse lifestyle, you know you're growing when it becomes second nature to clean out the stall, brush and feed your horse daily, and ride as often as you can.

When it comes to our spiritual lives, growing in truth means tapping into God's faith-building resources: having a daily quiet time, reading devotionals, and engaging in spiritual disciplines like Bible study, prayer, church, and sharing our faith. Personally connecting with God on a daily basis is essential to the life of every believer. God's Word is alive and active, and it will change our lives.

Truth isn't always easy to hear, but by accepting the lifestyle change that comes with the love of Jesus, we can receive the full benefit of having a relationship with Him.

Lord, help me to avoid spiritual junk food. I want the solid food of Your truth, amen.

61

Division in the Herd

If it is possible, as far as it depends on you, live at peace with everyone.
ROMANS 12:18

Horse herds work in community, and there is always a nervousness that comes with introducing a new horse to the group. Occasionally, we'll get a horse that just won't get along with others. A single horse can change the whole dynamic of our herd, causing restlessness and division.

A single person can cause restlessness and division too. It's sad to believe, but there are Christians out there who think it's their job to evaluate the holiness of other people. These folks have a hard time getting along with others and can change the entire dynamic when they're around. If you've ever been harshly criticized or judged by someone, you probably felt hurt and angry. That's normal.

However, the devil wants nothing more than to disintegrate our community with sin. He wants to divide our homes, marriages, businesses, and churches. He fans the flame of our hurt feelings, and he uses slander, grudges, and gossip to tear us apart.

Conflict happens in all our lives, but most conflicts could be contained or even fully resolved if believers would use Jesus' counsel that He offered in Matthew 18:15–17. In these verses, we see that God's Word leads us toward a goal of restoration instead of casting blame on others and living in bitterness or unforgiveness. Following the advice in the

Bible is the best way to stay in community, build each other up, and forgive one another.

Whatever you do, never fight with the critic, but instead keep your eyes on Jesus. Ask the Lord to reveal any truth in the criticism and to work on your faults. Then ask God to help you not to dwell on the person who hurt you but to forgive and love your brother or sister in Christ, because we have Jesus in common.

When handled correctly, our conflict can be an opportunity to strengthen relationships and shine for Jesus.

Lord, conflict is hard. Empower me to handle it with Your guidance, amen.

62

LET YOUR LIGHT SHINE

*"In the same way, let your light shine before others, that they may
see your good deeds and glorify your Father in heaven."*
MATTHEW 5:16

Horse shows are opportunities for horse and rider to show off all the fancy moves and difficult routines they've practiced for months. Riders dress in their finest, and horses are brushed, washed, and oiled until they gleam. The whole enterprise gives horses, riders, and owners a chance to shine before others.

Spiritually we also have an opportunity to shine. We believers are called to live out our faith in a dark world. Jesus said, "Let your light shine before others, that they may see your good deeds and glorify your Father in heaven." We may be the only representative of Christ that other people ever meet. Those around us will form an opinion about God based on our witness.

How are you shining? Do you keep to yourself or try to engage with others? Most of us are guilty of spending too much time with our smartphones or other devices that keep us away from a human connection. But if we don't take the time to interact with the world around us, we are going to miss out on the people God puts in our path for His purpose.

Ask God for help to truly *see* the people around you as go about your daily routine. When you drive to work, pray for wisdom to tune in to the heart-needs of coworkers and customers. If you work from home, try to get to know your neighbors. Are you a parent? Engage with your child's friends and their family members. Take time as you do errands to look in people's eyes and sincerely thank them if they're serving you. Little kindnesses could lead to conversations and eventually even relationships. As you notice needs and problems around you, offer God's hope and encouragement by listening with love and compassion.

Most of all, pray for courage to bring up the gospel when it's appropriate. As God leads, mention Jesus and what He's done for you. If you get nervous, remind yourself that the Holy Spirit resides in you and will help you obey the scriptural mandate to be a witness.

Shine on, friends!

Lord, please help me to let my light shine before others. I want to show Your glory in all I do, amen.

63

Unfair Perceptions

But Jesus said to them, "A prophet is not without honor except in his own town and in his own home." And he did not do many miracles there because of their lack of faith.
MATTHEW 13:57–58

Giving your trust to a horse after it has hurt you can be a hard obstacle to overcome. Even after a "naughty" horse has spent a good thirty days with a trainer, you are still left to wonder if he has changed his ways. The horse's behavior may have changed, but how we see him is still the same.

Horses aren't the only ones who suffer from unfair perceptions. Sometimes people's perceptions of us are hard to overcome. Even Jesus experienced this. When He traveled to His hometown of Nazareth, the people there still saw Him as a carpenter's son. Because they let pride blind their eyes, they missed out on the miracles the Messiah was willing to offer.

We also fall prey to people's old perceptions of us. After you become a new creation in Christ, it's the people you are closest to who have the hardest time recognizing and accepting the changed you. Don't get discouraged if you are labeled by the things you've done in your past. We all have a past we are not proud of, but Jesus took those sins of ours on Himself when He died on the cross. They no longer have any power over us.

"To follow Christ" means we apply the truths we learn from His Word (the Bible) and live as if Jesus were walking beside us in person. Don't make the mistake of seeking your validation and self-worth from the opinions of other people. Instead, know that the Father sees you as a new creation, which you are in Christ. Find your self-worth in knowing that you are God's beloved.

....

Lord, help me to see myself as You see me instead of finding my value in the opinions of others. Thank You that I am Your beloved, amen.

64

A CASE OF CHOKE

Devote yourselves to prayer, being watchful and thankful.
COLOSSIANS 4:2

M y horse Orlando feels he is entitled to his food, my food, and the food of the horse next to him. Because of his food aggression, he has sustained two leg injuries and a bad case of choke from trying to swallow grain before it was properly chewed.

Entitlement. It's a popular word in our culture today, and it has a way of darkening our hearts. If we're infected with this prideful mentality, we can feel entitled to unearned promotions, bigger houses, or even a better spouse. Entitlement even bleeds over into our spiritual lives, where we "church shop" for the congregation and worship service that will meet our needs instead of looking for the place God wants us to serve. Or we treat God as if He were a genie doling out wishes.

The truth is, we aren't entitled to anything from God. And He will refuse to fulfill our selfish demands. If we go into Christianity with the feeling that God owes us something, or if our measure of thanks to God is based on His "performance," then we are at risk of spiritual choke. God owes us nothing, but He *loves* us enough to give us His grace and mercy every day. God gives us what we need, and that's not always what we want.

Change your attitude by giving God your gratitude instead. And your heart will be filled with His light.

....

Lord, help me never to give in to an entitlement mentality. May I never take for granted the countless ways You have blessed me, amen.

65

FREE CHOICE

*Yet to all who did receive him, to those who believed in his name, he
gave the right to become children of God—children born not of natural
descent, nor of human decision or a husband's will, but born of God.*
JOHN 1:12–13

Whether it's because we lose our job, our health changes for the worse, or we experience a financial hardship, some of us will face the difficult decision of selling our horses. It can be excruciating to let go of an animal we've experienced joys and sorrows with. They become like a part of the family, and it is emotional to see them live somewhere else. Choosing to sell a horse can even cause us to want someone else to make our decisions. After all, wouldn't life be less complicated if we didn't have choices?

God gave us free will so we could make decisions. Otherwise, we would be like robots, only moving when He made us move. Free will is both a gift and a responsibility.

We have free will when it comes to love. Love is only love when it is voluntary. And we cannot freely and willingly give our hearts to God unless we have the option of *not* loving Him.

Jesus Christ gives us this choice when He stands at the door of our hearts and knocks. But we must open the door and ask Him to come into our lives. When you put your faith in Him and choose to follow Him, you become one of God's children.

Choose today to be His child for all eternity.

....

Lord, I choose You. Thank You for adopting me as a "child of God." Help me to grow in love with You more and more every day, amen.

66

PEACE BEYOND UNDERSTANDING

*And the peace of God, which surpasses all understanding,
will guard your hearts and your minds in Christ Jesus.*
PHILIPPIANS 4:7 ESV

T he worst part about owning a horse with navicular disease is witnessing how difficult it is for him to find peace due to his sore feet.
To a horse that's trying to rest, a comfy set of horseshoes can make all the
difference. Thankfully, farriers are constantly developing new ways to
make horses' feet more comfortable so the horses can be peaceful.

People, too, desire to find peace. It's hard for us to witness the life
of a person who does not have peace, or maybe it's you who would like
a life that is more surefooted and stable. Having peace when things are
going our way is exceedingly easy. But having peace during life's most
crippling moments can only happen when we read our Bible and stay in
communication with God. Knowing He is in control is the stable footing
that makes all the difference.

The disciples discovered this when they once got caught in a terrible
storm while they were crossing the lake in one of their fishing vessels.
Scared of drowning, they woke up Jesus, who had been sleeping through
the thunder and lightning, and accused Him of not caring for them.
"Save us!" they cried, their eyes wide with terror and fear choking their
voices. The Bible says, "He got up, rebuked the wind and said to the

waves, 'Quiet! Be still!' Then the wind died down and it was completely calm" (Mark 4:39).

Just as He did for the disciples, Jesus will bring calm to our wind-tossed lives when we trust Him completely. Keep in mind that the peace the Lord gives us is not the absence of chaos, but rather, the ability to stand firm when instability abounds. It's a peace that surpasses all human understanding.

Lord, I need an extra measure of peace today. Please give me peace that surpasses all human understanding, amen.

67

RIDING RIBBONS

The world and its desires pass away, but whoever
does the will of God lives forever.
1 JOHN 2:17

H orse shows are flat-out fun. The crowds and prizes involved in showing create an energy that's hard to match. Still, you don't measure the relationship you have with your horse by the number of riding ribbons you collect. Rather, we patiently pursue a long-term connection that is more about trust, patience, and overcoming challenges. We feed our horses, nurture them, and stay with them through the good and the bad times. In return, they give us companionship, love, and joy.

Careers, awards, and material things are all like show ribbons that fade over time. The things of this world will pass away, but God's love for us never fades. His love is so strong that He was willing to send His Son into the world to give His life for us.

So it makes sense that we should pursue those things that will last into eternity. Instead of spending untold hours seeking after fame and fortune, believers should spend time with God and find places to serve Him with their talents. As Jesus preached in his Sermon on the Mount, "But store up for yourselves treasures in heaven, where moths and vermin do not destroy, and where thieves do not break in and steal. For where your treasure is, there your heart will be also" (Matthew 6:20–21).

We pursue what we prize. Since Jesus could come back at any moment, shouldn't now be the time to live fully for God? Make peace what you pursue, and you will find Jesus every time.

....

Lord, forgive me for pursuing things that will ultimately fade and be turned to dust. I want to invest in the eternal instead, amen.

68

Start Clacking

All of you young people should obey your elders. In fact, everyone should be humble toward everyone else. . . . Be humble in the presence of God's mighty power, and he will honor you when the time comes.
1 Peter 5:5–6 CEV

F oals and younger horses display submissive behavior by lowering their heads and clacking their teeth together. By doing this, they are displaying a willingness to accept a lowly place among the herd.

For humans, shoveling manure could be considered the least desirable part of horse ownership—a definitely lowly task that keeps us humble. Yet it's a necessary way of serving our horses and keeping them healthy.

Submission. Humility. In this day and age, you'd think these were four-letter words. For Christ-followers, however, both are virtues that help us become more like Jesus and demonstrate servant leadership. Our Lord gave us an example of humility when He washed His disciples' feet. Even as the cross loomed in His mind, He bent His knees and took on the posture of a servant.

The submission that God asks of us does not imply lesser worth. He calls us to respect one another, depend willingly on someone else, and serve others. Humility before God is not complete unless there is also humility before man. God's perfect design for submission is a relationship that returns love for love, and service for service.

How can you serve your family, friends, and neighbors this week? Ask God for creative ideas on how to display humility. Then be willing to go through with the tasks He brings to mind.

And the next time your horse creates manure, remind yourself that your animal is keeping you humble. Come to think of it, if we all started clacking, what a wonderful world it would be.

....

Lord, I want to follow Your example of humility. Help me to return love for love and service for service, amen.

69

A Friend You Can Trust

*"I no longer call you servants, because a servant does not know his
master's business. Instead, I have called you friends, for everything
that I learned from my Father I have made known to you."*
JOHN 15:15

We riders often feel a mix of fear, insecurity, and excitement when trying a new horse: fear of making a wrong decision, insecurity about our riding skills, and excitement of the unknown.

People who don't follow Jesus, but feel drawn to Him, sometimes feel that same blend of fear, insecurity, and excitement. Maybe they're excited by what He offers but are afraid to give up a certain lifestyle, or they are insecure about their past choices and are fearful of His judgment. I have even heard some nonbelievers who say that they "tried Jesus" and it didn't work. But what they really meant to say was that they tried religion and it didn't work. Jesus is not a diet we can try or a worldview we can adopt. He's not a place we go or a phase we are going through.

Jesus is a friend we can trust. He invites us to come to Him at any time—just as we are—and He will never let us down. He listens to us, counsels us, and loves us unconditionally. Following Him as our friend means confessing with our mouths that He is our Lord and King and surrendering to Him as we turn from our sin. Trusting Him means accepting that what He has done for us on the cross makes us right with God.

Religion will leave you feeling dissatisfied and empty. Follow Jesus, and you will find an infallible friend.

....

Lord, I want to experience perfect love in my relationship with You. Help me to grow closer to You in friendship, amen.

70

GREENER PASTURES

He performs wonders that cannot be fathomed,
miracles that cannot be counted.
JOB 9:10

To horse people, springtime rain usually means mud, more mud, and lots more mud. But just when you think it will never stop raining, the sun comes out and your pasture sprouts green grass. Your horses kick up their heels and have renewed energy as temperatures warm and days get longer.

Just like the spring mud, our lives are messy and, at times, monotonous. If your life feels as though you are just spinning in mud, take a moment to think about how creative God is. We get so used to His creation, but what a miracle it is!

Study the intricately planned tilt of Earth and its orbit around the sun. We can count on God's handiwork as nature shows off its glory and diversity every day, every month, every year. God makes the sun come up and go down. He creates new snowflakes every winter and new flowers every spring. Rivers freeze and thaw; birds fly south for the winter and then migrate back as the seasons change. Animals hibernate in winter and then get frisky in spring. Small, cute new arrivals—foals, puppies, and rabbits—tug at our hearts.

The rain we sometimes moan about brings renewal to our world. Springtime gives and restores life.

What if, instead of griping about rain and mud, we opened our eyes to miracles, big and small? Fill your heart with His joy and His promises for greener pastures. It will change your perspective.

....

Lord, help me to see—and appreciate—Your miracles daily.
Help me to savor life, amen.

71

Put On Your Helmet

Take the helmet of salvation and the sword of
the Spirit, which is the word of God.
Ephesians 6:17

A great debate in the horse-riding community is over whether to ride with a helmet or not. There are many reasons why you should use a helmet, and plenty of reasons why some riders prefer not to. But just as other athletes protect their skulls against danger, horse riders, too, need protection for their heads.

As believers, we need protection against danger too. Not only are we guaranteed eternal life and fellowship with God when we accept Jesus' gift, but the Lord graciously gives us strong armor to keep us from being wounded in spiritual battles. And part of the armor God has given us is His Word. When we put on the helmet of salvation, we are putting on protection that the enemy cannot penetrate.

Make no mistake, the enemy is after our minds. Sometimes our thoughts can deceive us—such as when negative untruths swirl through our brains: *you are worthless, you are not good enough, you will never make a difference,* or *you will never do anything significant.* When thoughts like these invade our minds, we need to remind ourselves of the central truth of the gospel: Jesus loves us so much that He died for us. The untruths

Satan hurls at us are no match for the generous sacrifice and precious promises of our loving Savior.

Guard and protect against the schemes of the enemy by putting on your helmet and applying the salvation you have been given. The Bible is your weapon, waiting to be used. So take control and defend yourself by opening its pages. Put God's miracles to work in your mind.

....

Lord, thank You for providing protection from Satan. Help me daily to put on my spiritual armor, amen.

72

Growing in Trust

The LORD is trustworthy in all he promises and faithful in all he does.
PSALM 145:13

T he key to any relationship is trust, and it is particularly important when it comes to horses. We have all had that moment when we want a horse to trust us, but we aren't getting the same commitment in return. In those moments of rejection, we can begin to imagine how God must feel when we don't trust Him.

Despite His faithfulness to His promises and His never-changing character, some people still reject the idea that God is trustworthy. Maybe they have experienced unanswered prayers or tragedies from which they felt God should have spared them. Or maybe they have a wrong perception of God from their childhoods or a false teacher. Whatever the reasons, the Bible repeatedly stresses that God is completely trustworthy and faithful. Scripture is a picture of a loving, patient, and radically merciful God who will stop at nothing to have relationship with the people He created.

The truth is, you cannot trust someone you don't know. So getting to know Him is the key to learning how to trust Him. Also, as we walk in communion with Him, we learn that He has our best interests at heart, even when He doesn't answer our prayers on our schedule or says no to a prayer.

If you are having trouble trusting in God's character and goodness, tell Him so. He already knows how you feel, and He longs for a genuine connection with you. Don't be afraid to converse honestly with Him. Treat Him like the friend He is, and He will make Himself known to you.

Lord, I confess I sometimes have trouble trusting You. Give me the courage to be honest. As I open up to You, show Yourself to me in new ways, amen.

73

HE SEEKS THE LOST

*Jesus said, . . . "There is more happiness in heaven because of one sinner
who turns to God than over ninety-nine good people who don't need to."*
LUKE 15:7 CEV

New-horse shopping is always an enchanting adventure. But as exciting as it is, the best advice I have ever received on horse buying is this: be patient when seeking a horse, and the right one will find you.

In Christianity, God seeks after people, as opposed to other religions where people attempt to find God. Jesus came to seek the lost. He once told a story in which a shepherd with one hundred sheep had one lamb who got lost. Devastated, the shepherd left the ninety-nine sheep in the field to go out and search for the one lost sheep. When the shepherd found the animal, he put it on his shoulders and carried it home. Then the shepherd called his friends and neighbors and threw a party, celebrating the return of the wayward lamb.

We are the lost lamb in the story, and Jesus is the shepherd. Think about just how important we are to God. It is hard to fathom.

Our heavenly Father is patient with all who are not yet saved, desiring that no one perish (2 Peter 3:9). He seeks after these pre-believers like a shepherd searching for his lost animal. And when even one lost soul is found, heaven rejoices!

The next time you wonder about your worth or feel insecure, think about the story of the lost sheep. You are incredibly valuable to the Creator of the universe. Let Him find you.

....

Lord, I'm so grateful You are patient and loving. Thank You for never giving up on finding me, amen.

74

Paid in Full

*Know then in your heart that as a man disciplines his
son, so the LORD your God disciplines you.*
DEUTERONOMY 8:5

M uch like everything else having to do with horses, *discipline* is a topic that seems open to much debate. Where is the line between breaking a horse's spirit and teaching him manners?

Some trainers discipline harshly, while others are more gentle in their approaches. Both methods have their proponents, but I have found that building trust—and a relationship—with my horses over time works better than punishing them.

When we have hard days, months, or even years, we sometimes wonder if God is punishing us for the wrong choices we have made in our lives. But there is a difference between punishment and discipline. Yes, God allows difficult seasons in our lives in order that we might mature in our faith and bring glory to Him, and sometimes sin brings natural and spiritual consequences. Our heavenly Father doesn't try to break our spirits with hard times; rather, He uses them to teach us how to live as children of God.

God's punishment for our sin has already been dealt with when Jesus was nailed to the cross. And because He gave everything to set us free from sin and death, we can trust Him. We see how far He has gone in pursuing a relationship with us, and that allows us to come near to Him without fear.

While there will be consequences—and sometimes God's loving discipline—for the things we do here on earth, you can sleep well at night knowing your punishment for sin has been paid in full.

....

Lord, thank You for Your loving, consistent discipline, amen.

75

HORSE PEOPLE

*We proclaim to you what we have seen and heard, so that
you also may have fellowship with us. And our fellowship
is with the Father and with his Son, Jesus Christ.*

1 JOHN 1:3

Horse people are a set all their own. Not only do I value the friendships I have with my horses, but I'm also grateful for the friendships of the horse people around me. When life bucks us off, it's nice to have someone there to pick us up off the ground. My horse buddies are the ones hitching up their trailers and preparing to go the distance for me and my ponies.

When our horses are sick, we are there for one another with wraps, medicines, or any other supplies that are needed. (Much like parenting, it seems that medical catastrophes with horses only happen on weekends or after dark!) Also, horse people help trailer each other's horses when we need to. And we board one another's animals when big catastrophes like barn fires or hurricanes strike.

It's natural for us to want to be around people who love and support us. As Christians, we need to hitch up our trailers with other believers in fellowship.

If you are in fellowship, then you are in the perfect place for ministering to the needs of other Christians, sharpening one another's faith and encouraging each other. To help keep our paths shining bright, it's all about the company we keep.

Some people are reluctant to join a church family or a Bible study group. Maybe they're afraid of getting hurt or are nervous about sharing their journey with fellow believers. No church is perfect, because churches are made up of all-too-human folks, but God created us to function as a body of Christ. We need one another.

If you've received Christ as your personal Savior and Lord, you are a member of God's family. So let's hitch up our spiritual trailers together, and go the distance for one another.

....

Lord, thank You for the fellowship I have with other believers, amen.

76

<hr>

Don't Put God in a Box

*Now to him who is able to do immeasurably more than all we ask
or imagine, according to his power that is at work within us.*
EPHESIANS 3:20

S hetland ponies have long, thick manes and tails and a dense, double winter coat. Because of their unique design, they can withstand all types of harsh weather. They would rather be outside. Despite knowing this, I sometimes give in to the urge to stall my ponies during storms. By not trusting God's design, I am putting my ponies in a box.

Because of our limited thinking, we can sometimes forget that God can do immeasurably more than we ask. We are so focused on the goodness of God that we forget He is mighty. He desires to do exceedingly, abundantly beyond all that we can think or imagine.

Through the ages, the nature and character of God has been described in countless ways—holy, compassionate, merciful, gracious, loving, faithful, and forgiving, to name a few. Yet as pastor Charles Stanley pointed out in his book, *A Gift of Love*, there is one essential character trait that all humanity can celebrate—*giving*: "We have life only because God has created us by an exercise of His will. We can receive salvation only because He wills to grant it."[3]

God's ever-giving heart allows us to approach Him. Incredibly, our voices matter in heaven. Let's not make the mistake of putting limitations on God. That's like putting Him into a box. Instead, remember that we serve a mighty, giving God.

....

Lord, help me never to put You in a box or doubt Your ever-giving heart, amen.

77

THE ONE TRUE THING

For I resolved to know nothing while I was with you
except Jesus Christ and him crucified.
1 CORINTHIANS 2:2

S ometimes when we get around horse people, we find ourselves surrounded by all kinds of know-it-alls. And in some cases, they actually do. The equine educated can make us feel like inadequate equestrians at times. But that's when we remind ourselves of what is most important: we love our horses, and our horses trust us.

What's more, it can be so tempting to compare ourselves to other riders. But we will never succeed at being ourselves if we are trying to be someone else.

Our spiritual journey is our own too. When we are tempted to compare ourselves with other Christians, we should focus instead on the Lord. He is the One we are following. "Each one should test their own actions. Then they can take pride in themselves alone, without comparing themselves to someone else" (Galatians 6:4).

The truth is, we will meet other Christians along the trail who seem to know every Bible verse, have theology degrees, and speak eloquent prayers. And it's easy to feel intimidated by a person with that kind of intellect. Remember: all that matters is that *you* know the one thing that is most important: "Jesus Christ and him crucified." If you know that, then you know the most important thing of all.

....

Lord, help me to avoid the temptation of comparing myself with others. Help me to hold on to the one true thing: my relationship with You, amen.

78

HUSH, HUSH

If we confess our sins, he is faithful and just and will forgive
us our sins and purify us from all unrighteousness.
1 JOHN 1:9

S *trangles* happens! This contagious sickness is an upper respiratory
infection. The horse's lymph nodes swell and compress his pharynx, larynx, and trachea. It can even cause airway obstruction (hence the
name) and death. My horse Sven had Strangles, and he was quarantined
for two months. Nobody came to ride with me because if people hear
your horse has Strangles, they avoid your barn as though you have the
plague—and you kind of do.

Aside from the isolation, the hardest part about having Strangles
in my barn is admitting that my horse has it. Some horse owners are
so "hush, hush" about this disease that their silence contributes to the
spread of it.

In our spiritual lives, we often try to cover up sin. But sin happens. And trying to hide it only contributes to the spread of it. Sin, for a
believer, strangles our relationship with God. In some instances, it can
cause us to run away from Him. Often, others are affected by our wrong
choices too. They might even be tempted to fall into certain sins because
we've done so.

It's as if there's a tug-of-war going on inside us. We want to do what's right; we want to please God—yet we find ourselves giving into temptation. Then, instead of coming clean, we turn away from the only One who can fully restore us. And we bring our friends down with us.

If this describes you, guess what: you're not alone. Even one of the great heroes of the faith, the apostle Paul, agonized with you: "I do not understand what I do. For what I want to do I do not do, but what I hate I do" (Romans 7:15).

Christians do not have to keep asking for forgiveness for the same sins—that includes past, present, and future. But by confessing your sin to God and ceasing from doing it, you will be restored in your relationship with God who loves you and has already forgiven you.

Don't get strangled by sin. Instead, keep a clean conscience and a healthy connection to God. Then the only thing contagious about you will be your faith.

Lord, thank You for Your forgiveness. Thank You for victory over sin, amen.

79

Cleaning Out Our Spiritual Tack Room

*Do not conform to the pattern of this world, but be
transformed by the renewing of your mind.*
Romans 12:2

I always seem to have substantially more tack than I need. I have bridles, bits, saddles, and other accessories for days. Why is tack so addictive? And why do I collect more of it than I even have space for? If I didn't clean my tack room out on occasion, I wouldn't have any room left in the barn for my horses. But as cluttered as it gets, my mind gets ever more so.

As social media, current events, and opinions invade our lives, it's tempting to let negative thoughts collect in our minds. The daily news—with its market fluctuations, natural disasters, and political infighting—can overwhelm our faith in very little time. And a steady diet of godless television programs, movies, and music can bring us down emotionally, mentally, and spiritually.

If we allow it to, this kind of junk-food diet can affect our thoughts to the point that we are no longer reflecting Christ in our actions. By cleaning out our spiritual tack rooms daily, we can make a choice to stay renewed by Christ instead. Prayer, Bible study, church attendance, and worship are some of the ways to live His way.

When we stay saturated with His Word instead of being ensnared by media hype and useless information, we can keep the culture and its negativity from creeping back in. Let's be "addicted" to God and the Bible instead of to worldly things. Then our lives will be so full of Him that the world won't be able to influence us.

Lord, clean out my spiritual tack room. Help me to feast on Your Word and not ingest too much of the world, amen.

80

MUSIC TO GOD'S EARS

Come, let us sing for joy to the LORD; let us shout aloud
to the Rock of our salvation. Let us come before him with
thanksgiving and extol him with music and song.
PSALM 95:1–2

Although my patient neighbors may disagree with my musical tastes, in my opinion all donkeys have perfect pitch.

I once critiqued the music at church and was offered the sober reminder that I am not there to be entertained but to worship the Lord. Coincidently, that would also be one of the many occasions in which I was caught acting like a donkey.

If the sound system buzzes and no one's in tune, does that mean they worship less? What about when the worship ministry uses modern choruses backed by drums, guitars, and keyboards while you prefer hymns with piano and organ accompaniment? *Any* kind of heartfelt worship is music to God's ears.

So many of the issues we argue about are preferences. However, in our humanness, we tend to get dogmatic and easily offended when people disagree with our tastes.

Scholar and author Leonard Sweet recently wrote on his Facebook page about researching the issues his Methodist denomination had argued about more than 150 years ago. One of the main controversies was "promiscuous seating" at church. In other words, Methodists were arguing over whether families, including children, should sit together in worship. For many years, men had sat on one side while women and children sat on the other. Sweet noted, "In 1847, [this issue] was causing splits in churches and charges of heresy, tearing apart communities. . . . So I wonder . . . how many of our holy hullabaloos today will look just as ridiculous 100 or 150 or 170 years from now?"[4]

Whether it's controversy about music style or another aspect of church life, let's not allow dissension over nonessentials. After all, church isn't about pleasing ourselves; it's about being in tune with the Lord.

Lord, forgive me when I stir dissension over nonessentials. Help me concentrate on things that matter to You, amen.

81

PUNY PRAYERS

Finally, be strong in the Lord and in his mighty power.
EPHESIANS 6:10

As I mentioned earlier, nothing gets my mind reeling and my heart pumping more than a Strangles diagnosis in a horse that lives among a herd of other horses. This happened to my horses one time. After quarantining the one, I found myself praying, "When the others fall victim to this contagious illness, please let it go quickly." With no other horses showing symptoms a week later, I finally discovered that Strangles was never my issue at all, but rather that I was praying puny prayers to a mighty God.

As believers, we often limit ourselves by our own small prayers. God is more than capable of doing far beyond anything we can even comprehend. So why do we pray for wimpy things like parking spaces instead of being bold and imaginative in our prayers?

We have access to the One who is infinitely more powerful than anything in the world. God's power is dynamic, energetic, mighty, and strong. Think about the first line in Scripture: "In the beginning God created the heavens and the earth" (Genesis 1:1). Wow. This same God is alive in you and me, and He bends to hear our requests.

The power of the almighty God raised Christ from the dead, and it can change human hearts. It sets addicts free from their sinful habits, restores relationships, gives hope to the hopeless, and it's available to every believer. Because of Christ's power, no sinner is beyond rescue.

Whatever you are facing today, call down the power of heaven with your prayers. God is *mighty*!

Lord, forgive me for praying puny prayers. Help me to approach You boldly, amen.

82

GET MOVING

Put on the full armor of God, so that you can take
your stand against the devil's schemes.
EPHESIANS 6:11

Horse owners know that when their equine companions get sick, it's best not to let them lie down for long periods of time. While there is no rule about how long a horse can be down before permanent damage ensues, the sooner you can get them moving, the better.

We, too, tend to lie down when things get tough. One of the ways Satan lies to us is that he tries to convince us that our lives would be easier if we would just lie down and quit. That's when God urges us to keep moving forward, one faithful step after another. Life is hard, even if we love Jesus. And the longer we lie down and believe the schemes of the devil, the longer we are not working for God.

Do you feel powerless to fight Satan? You're not. God has given us practical and powerful weapons to protect us and thwart our enemy's plans. He has given us a shield of faith that we can use at any time. Next time you are tempted to give in to despair or hopelessness, say out loud, "Satan, you are a liar. I believe in Jesus, and His blood covers me. You have no authority here!"

God has also provided us with the sword of truth—the Bible. When you feel attacked by insecurity or discouragement, find scriptures that tell you of your worth in Christ. Say them—out loud, if possible—and claim their truths over the enemy's lies and your roller-coaster emotions.

Before damage ensues, get up and move. In the seasons of life that make it hard for us to stand up, remind yourself that you are standing behind the God of the universe. His armor gives you all you need to battle spiritual forces.

Lord, I will put on the full armor and will keep fighting. Go before me and guide me, amen.

83

GOD'S MASTERPIECE

You are the one who put me together inside my mother's body, and
I praise you because of the wonderful way you created me.
PSALM 139:13–14 CEV

I f I were to add up all the hours I think about my horses, I'm sure it
would total an embarrassing chunk of my day. I think about where
we'll ride next time, how much and when I need to feed them, and how
blessed I feel to have such warm and affectionate animal friends. I plan
our next road trip, think about the treats I'll get at the store next time I'm
in town, and look through catalogs of bridles, bits, and other horse gear.

We think about the things we care about the most, so it's no surprise
to know that God thinks about us constantly. He's like a proud Father
who can't stop talking about His children. Not only does God love us,
care for us, and rejoice over us with singing (Zephaniah 3:17), but we are
the recipients of His grace. His love is something we could never earn
or deserve, and yet He gives it freely. Not only that, but the Psalms also
speak of us being the masterpiece of God's creation (8:5) and the apple
of His eye (17:8). Just imagine—of all the incredible animals, plants, and
stars, *we* are His favorite. What a stunning truth.

We tend to expect so little in life. Meanwhile, the God of the universe
has incredible regard for each one of us. God truly loves us more than

we can comprehend. And He's not embarrassed at all by how much He thinks about us.

....

Thank You for making each of us a masterpiece. Help me never to forget how valuable I am to You, amen.

84

Packing Your Saddlebags

If you declare with your mouth, "Jesus is Lord," and believe in your
heart that God raised him from the dead, you will be saved.
Romans 10:9

hen it comes to trail riding, there is never an assurance that everything will go smoothly along the route. So many things can go
wrong. My horse could buck me off, a piece of equipment could malfunc-
tion, or I could get lost or hurt. And just in case of trouble, my saddlebags
are always heaping full of items to help me navigate the what-ifs: my
pocket knife, water bottle, cell phone, and a leather punch.

We will encounter plenty of uncertainties along the trail of life as
well. But when you accept Christ as your Lord and believe God raised
Him from the dead, you are packing your saddlebags with something you
can be sure about: your salvation. The assurance of our salvation is in the
unprejudiced truth of God's Word. We should not live our Christian lives
wondering and worrying each day whether we are truly saved. God said
we *are*—and that is enough.

In fact, part of our spiritual armor is called "the helmet of salvation"
(Ephesians 6:17). The work Christ did on the cross is sufficient for not
only saving us from eternal separation from God, but also surviving the
fiery darts of the enemy.

When the devil tries to accuse you of not being saved, remind him of his defeat at the tomb. Tell him that Jesus already beat him, and he has no business bringing up old wounds. Use Scripture to banish him from your presence.

God has given each of us the tools we need to navigate the trails of life. It's up to us to use them.

....

Lord, thank You for the promise that my salvation is secure. Because I've put my trust in You and turned from my sins, I don't have to worry anymore, amen.

85

RIDE STRONG

I can do all things through Christ who strengthens me.
PHILIPPIANS 4:13 NKJV

R iding competitions have a way of highlighting our strengths but also our weaknesses. And if you are smart, you will use the critical information the judges give you to make your next ride even stronger. They may have advice about how to execute a walk or trot better, or they may correct your balance or your contact with the horse.

In the same way, difficult times reveal our strengths and our weaknesses. Trials in life can make our hearts feel tired. We know that God is in control, but some days it is hard to live it. The enemy strikes us where we are weakest, especially if we are already suffering with something else.

When you are under attack, the Holy Spirit can help strengthen your places of weakness.

For instance, I ask the Holy Spirit for wisdom in parenting because my kids are so different from each other. If I am uneasy about a parenting decision, I usually can reason that it's the Holy Spirit warning me about that situation. And when I am about to react to something my child said, I try to run it by the Spirit first.

There are also times the Spirit gives me the strength to do something I know must be done, such as when I once had to let an employee go.

There were legitimate reasons, but I still struggled with the decision. In the end, the Spirit helped me make the choice I needed to make.

Praying to the Holy Spirit for strength can make our rides stronger. It lets us emerge from our struggles more Christlike than before.

....

Lord, I know that I can do all things through You. And right now, I need Your strength, amen.

86

LET GO AND FORGIVE

"For if you forgive other people when they sin against you, your
heavenly Father will also forgive you. But if you do not forgive
others their sins, your Father will not forgive your sins."
MATTHEW 6:14–15

I t's easy to forgive my horses for their faults. Most of the time, if something is off, it's because of something I did, not because of something they are intentionally or selfishly doing. People, however, are harder for me to forgive. This struggle to forgive is one of the hardest parts about being a Christian. In moments of frustration toward a family member, coworker, or friend, it's easier to remember all the wrongs he or she has done to us.

Forgiveness is not excusing or condoning a person's bad behavior. Instead, it's choosing to let go of the anger that can make you bitter and then giving the whole situation over to God to handle. In fact, God puts such a high priority on forgiveness that He *commands* believers to forgive others.

Now, you might wonder why the Bible says—such as in today's scripture—that God won't forgive us if we do not forgive the sins of others. It seems contradictory to God's merciful character as shown through the cross. However, our heavenly Father knows what is best for us. Holding grudges, becoming angry, and harboring bitterness can lead to strained relationships, stress, and health problems. Over time, those habits can even change our personalities. We've all met people who have let negativity and hatefulness infuse their hearts until they can't see straight. None of us wants to end up like that.

The next time you feel tempted not to forgive, think of all the sins God has forgiven you for. Thank Him for His grace, and ask Him for help to let go and move on.

Lord, thank You for Your forgiveness. Help me to forgive others, amen.

87

THE LEADERSHIP OF OUR LIVES

*Love the LORD your God with all your heart and with
all your soul and with all your strength.*
DEUTERONOMY 6:5

S ome people view horses as willful beasts not capable of exhibiting loyalty or reasonable behavior. These people often deal with horses by using extreme force until the human breaks the horse's spirit. Ruling a horse with fear is not only unjustifiable but also unnecessary, because horses can easily become willing partners if they are shown kindness, patience, and compassion.

Some Christians use fear as a tactic to try and scare people into the kingdom of God. Whether it's a deathbed confession or a lifetime of servanthood, committing to Christ is transferring leadership of our lives over to God. God does not want you to submit to Him out of fear but rather to come to Him out of love, willingly.

The good news is that if you have breath, you are never too far gone or too dirty for Jesus. When you put your faith and trust in Jesus, God promises to forgive you and give you the gift of eternal life. Are you ready to turn ownership of your life over to Him and become a willing partner? Would you like to commit to Him right *now*? There is not a specific prayer in scripture you must pray, so something along the lines of the following will work just fine. Pray it to God with all your heart:

Dear God, I know that I am a sinner. I believe that Jesus Christ, Your Son, died on the cross for my sin and rose from the dead to be my Lord. God, I now repent of my sin and personally invite Jesus into my life. Thank You, Jesus for giving me the free gift of eternal life. I promise to live for You as You reveal Yourself to me through Your Word, the Bible. In Jesus' name, I pray, amen.

Welcome to the family of Christ!

....

Lord, thank You for giving me the freedom to choose You willingly. Help me to serve and please You with my life, amen.

88

Horse Rookie

*"You will be hated by everyone because of me, but the
one who stands firm to the end will be saved."*
MATTHEW 10:22

When you start loving horses, it's all about loving horses and anything involving horses. However, because we're rookies, we tend to doubt ourselves. We look to others for validation, instead of being secure in what we know.

As a newbie in carriage driving, I was told by my instructor that I needed an overcheck for my horse. This is a piece of horse tack that runs from a point on the horse's back, over the head to a bit, and is designed to keep your horse's head up. I did not feel right about this piece of equipment for my horse Gus, but my instructor had a very bold personality. I didn't want to disagree with her out of fear she would treat me negatively. I called a carriage-driving store and inquired about it, only to be told that this piece of equipment was cruel. I am so thankful that the person on the other end of the phone had the guts to tell me what I knew deep down but was unwilling to say. I am also thankful I found a new instructor.

Even in the spiritual realm, we often look to others for acceptance instead of focusing on God alone. I wasn't raised in the church, which means that growing up, I never knew about a God who loved me, cared about me, and had a plan for my life. I was silently seeking Jesus, but I was also afraid people would reject me or label me a Bible thumper for believing. As it turns out, all that time I struggled with my search for God, He was seeking me.

Don't make the mistake of seeking your validation and self-worth from the opinions of others. If you long to obey Jesus, but you're afraid of how people will label you if you surrender, don't let the fear of rejection be your snare. Remember the passion you felt when you first came to Christ, and how simple and pure your love was? Don't look for others to accept you. Instead, seek God's wisdom and approval, and you'll rest secure in His peace.

Lord, forgive me for looking to others for validation. Keep me focused on You alone, amen.

89

HIDDEN TREASURE

*But we have this treasure in jars of clay to show that this
all-surpassing power is from God and not from us.*
2 CORINTHIANS 4:7

From newborn foals to equine geriatrics, each one of my horses has brought principles—and people—into my life that have enhanced my relationship with God. Some of my horses have been those no one else wanted. If God had wanted to, He certainly could have reached me without these horses, but He chose an unlikely group of broken-down horses to teach me. I have found beautiful parables in the faces and sway-backed bodies of these horses that some would call worthless.

The world can make us feel as if we are worthless, but God values us. And He uses us, but we must make ourselves available to Him. No one is too young or too small, too old or in too much trouble. Cover to cover, the Bible is chock-full of misfits chosen by God to do His divine work: Moses stuttered. Joseph was hated by his brothers. David was an adulterer. Jonah ran away when God called him to preach. Jacob was a thief and a liar. Samson was impatient and arrogant.

He used these broken-down people so it was clear that the power came from God and not them. Just look at me: I have a reading comprehension problem and a twelfth-grade education, so why not make me a writer? What an unlikely choice!

When God chooses to use the unqualified, He makes it clear that our great power is from Him and not from ourselves. If you are allowing excuses to keep you from working for God, then it's time for you to reconsider the mission and start trusting in Him. If you give God your availability, He will give you the ability.

Lord, I'm one of those misfits who wants to serve You. Empower me and give me Your strength, amen.

90

Farm Calls

"It is not the healthy who need a doctor, but the sick. I
have not come to call the righteous, but sinners."
Mark 2:17

S ometimes during emergencies it's impossible to get a horse into the
vet clinic. A farm call will bring the vet clinic to you. In our darkest hours of equine ownership, there is an overwhelming comfort that
comes when you hear your veterinarian say, "I am on my way!"

Jesus often went to people's houses too. He was often criticized for
dining with the spiritually sick. The Pharisees noticed this and asked
why He ate with tax collectors and sinners. Jesus simply responded that
He had not come to call the righteous, but sinners. Consider what the
Great Physician's message would look like if He were never willing to
make house calls. His example encourages us to rub elbows with the
people who need Him the most.

We build our churches with the expectation that hurting people will
walk through the door. But the Lord instructs us to go out into the world.
That's often where the people who are spiritually lonely are.

Living our lives in a holy huddle with other Christians makes us feel
safe—even comfortable. When our focus is on the huddle, we don't have
to deal with scary people on the outside. But here's some amazing news:
our comfort has a low biblical priority.

Jesus calls us to spend time *out* of our holy huddles and to impact the world for Him. Throughout the Gospels, we see examples of Christ making His disciples uncomfortable by befriending scary people—outcasts.

Are you sharing God's love with those around you? What do people see when they look at your life? Humility, kindness, goodness—a reflection of Christ's face? This is a great time to start making house calls.

Lord, teach me to make heavenly house calls. I, too, want to share the good news with those around me. Give me opportunities to be Your witness, amen.

91

Lost and Found

*"There is joy in the presence of the angels of
God over one sinner who repents."*
Luke 15:10 NRSV

Fly spray, buckets, and brushes are just some of the basic barn items that I replace far too often. Usually, my trip to the store happens after I've returned home from a riding event. We horse people label everything because at horse competitions these types of items seem to grow legs and wander away.

Losing something makes us anxious, especially when that something is useful or valuable. When these lost objects become found, we share our relief with friends. That is how God views us—as that wandering someone who needs to be found. God rejoices over every lost sinner who repents. In Luke 15, Jesus told a parable about a woman who had ten silver coins. She lost one, so she turned on the lights, got out her broom, and searched high and low until she found the misplaced coin. Then she called her friends and neighbors to tell them the good news.

Even though we may feel small and insignificant at times, we are loved by God. He sees us as valuable, and He searched for us until we were no longer lost. Amazingly, all of heaven rejoices for us.

Scripture reminds us to focus on the Lord and to recognize that

Christians have the key to a significant, marvelous, joyful, and fulfilling life. It's all grounded in a relationship with Jesus Christ.

You were once lost, but now you're found.

....

Lord, thank You that I am no longer lost. Thank You that my life matters to You, amen.

92

DONKEYS VERSUS HORSES

*"So when you give to the needy, do not announce it with trumpets, as the
hypocrites do in the synagogues and on the streets, to be honored by others."*
MATTHEW 6:2

Just as with most of my free-to-a-good-home horses, one spring I
was fortunate enough to be given two donkeys. Other than the fact
that they have four legs and a horse-shaped face, I have discovered that
donkeys are nothing like horses at all. In other words, they may look
like a horse, but they act like a donkey. These kind, affectionate, and
intelligent animals are loud when they bray, but when you pet them, they
almost purr.

While both horses and donkeys are social, horses like to group into
packs, but donkeys will often bond with just one other donkey. Horses
are also easier to scare than donkeys. And donkeys' tails and manes are
stiffer and more brittle than horses' tails and manes.

Just as donkeys and horses look similar but are very different, there
is often quite a difference between people who merely say they're Christ-
followers and those who actually are. Just because people call themselves
Christians doesn't mean they are good representations of the real thing.
They may have two legs, attend church regularly, and quote Scripture
with the best of them, but they are not following Jesus. These "donkeys"
are not what Jesus intended His followers to be like.

The world is full of Christians who profess to know Jesus but do it so crudely that people around them think loving Jesus makes you unloving of others. How sad that to some people, the definition of *Christian* includes the words *mean*, *hypocritical*, or *phony*.

You will never stop encountering the self-righteous, but it would be a terrible shame if you allowed them to be the only vocal and bold representatives of Jesus.

Lord, I don't want to be a donkey. Remove hypocrisy and phoniness from my life. Mold me into the person You desire me to be, amen.

93

Strong and Flexible

*Paul and his companions traveled throughout the region of
Phrygia and Galatia, having been kept by the Holy Spirit
from preaching the word in the province of Asia.*
ACTS 16:6

W hen foals are born, their legs are 90 percent of their adult length. The big, strong, and flexible design of these newborn legs enables them to stand and run alongside their mothers just hours after birth. It's comical to watch foals bend their long legs to reach even the tallest grass.

Flexibility is a blessing to foals, but it applies to our Christian lives too. It's okay to make plans for our future. However, we should remain flexible and continually listen to God's voice so we are prepared to change our plans when He sends us off in another direction. Today's scripture highlights the need to take actions based on whether it is the Lord's will or not. The apostle Paul was going to preach in Asia, but he changed his plans when the Holy Spirit made it clear he was not to do that. Paul and his companions instead traveled throughout a different region.

As Christ-followers, we can become so preoccupied or even arrogant that we shift from confidence in Jesus Christ to reliance on our own intellect. We should instead rely on the Holy Spirit to guide us. Even when we don't understand why He's changing our plans, we need to remain open and obedient. Just as a foal will eventually grow into his legs, when we continue to commit our plans to God, we will continue to grow toward the goal He has designed for us.

Comprehending God's plan can wait; obeying God's will cannot.

....

Lord, I want Your plan for my life. Help me to be flexible as I build on the solid foundation of faith, amen.

94

Between Two Horses

Let the peace of Christ rule in your hearts, to which indeed
you were called in one body. And be thankful.
Colossians 3:15 esv

I f we are unaware of our surroundings when we're with horses, we could put ourselves in the riskiest place there is to be—between two horses. Horse behavior is unpredictable, and two seemingly friendly horses can come unhinged by something as simple as a swinging bucket or a floating flake of hay. There is no scarier feeling than when you are caught standing in the middle.

I spent many years of my life caught in the middle between belief in God and not really knowing Him. Although I deeply desired a relationship with Jesus, I had a tough time trusting Him. It wasn't until I learned I was not in control—and that I was broken—that my faith began to grow.

A few years ago, I was sick and didn't know what was going on. When I was told I needed to be checked for colon cancer, I felt the air go out of me and immediately thought about my kids having to watch me go through cancer treatment. But then I read the Bible verse, "Cast all your anxiety on him" (1 Peter 5:7), and I understood that none of this had anything to do with me. Instead, it was about how I use my life to bring glory to God. The test came back fine, but my experience carried me from being more of a casual believer into growing in a relationship with God. I wasn't in the middle anymore.

What are you holding on to? Are you caught between faith and trust? Cast your fear on the Lord. Surrender to God, and allow His peace to wash over you and His promises to preserve you.

Lord, I don't want to be stuck in that in-between place. I want to know You intimately. Remove the doubt in my life. Help me to trust You, amen.

95

Runaway Stagecoach

*See to it that no one falls short of the grace of God and that no
bitter root grows up to cause trouble and defile many.*
Hebrews 12:15

Y"ou can't sit through an entire western movie without experiencing the spills and thrills of the stagecoach chase. The drama in these pictures usually builds throughout the first half of the movie and ends with a climactic runaway stagecoach. Of course, there are ways to stop the stagecoach by just shooting the horses pulling it, but that also ends the movie with no hero left to praise.

Consider this: wallowing in self-righteous anger is like being trapped on a runaway stagecoach. Resentment starts when we perceive a situation as unfair or feel mistreated by another person. Over time, the melodramas in our minds begin to play, reminding us of all the hurtful things we'd like to say to that person. Just as the speed of the stagecoach keeps increasing, so do our feelings of injustice. But the reality is, the enemy would like nothing more than to see us barreling toward a cliff and ultimately spiraling down to our death.

Resentment is *all* emotion and the devil's favorite play. The choice is ours: keep blaming others, or break the cycle. Injustice is a part of this fallen world, but by concentrating on who we are in Christ, we will facilitate our own heart change.

During those moments when you find bitterness taking control of your stagecoach, praise the Lord instead, and be rescued by our greatest hero, Jesus Christ.

....

Lord, please clear away any resentment in my heart. Heal the hurt and restore peace, amen.

96

Predictably Unpredictable

Answer me when I call to you, my righteous God. Give me relief
from my distress; have mercy on me and hear my prayer.
Psalm 4:1

As much as we try to fix and control our environment when it comes to riding horses, most things are out of our control. The only thing we can say with complete certainty about horses is that they are predictably unpredictable. And we can easily find ourselves on the ground after a horse loses its footing or jolts.

God can be unpredictable too. When He answers our prayers, it's not always in ways we expect.

Sometimes He takes us out of our comfort zone to give us a better perspective on the thing we thought we wanted. For example, I prayed for patience, and God allowed me to have a health scare, which I told you about in a previous devotion. Maybe you've said a prayer about the person you wanted to marry or the dream job you thought you needed, and God's answer jolted you. Perhaps He said no or "wait" instead of yes. God doesn't always answer us in the time frame we expect or think we deserve.

His delays or denials are frustrating and emotionally difficult. We can even lose hope and feel that God doesn't truly care. But remember, God sees the big picture and ultimately delivers us to the things that are best for us. So often we can't see things clearly when we are in the middle of our circumstances.

And it's possible that God has answered a prayer in a way that we may never know about until we get to heaven. We can ask God to do things our way and repair situations as we think best, yet His wisdom is much higher than ours. Thanking God for the answered prayers and miracles in our past is a good way to remind ourselves that God always comes through for us, even when it's in ways we can't see or understand.

God will never stop being good, so don't stop being grateful.

....

Lord, I don't always sense answers to my prayers, but I know You care and are listening. Help me to understand that You are working things out in Your perfect time, amen.

97

FINISH WELL

Something completed is better than something just begun.
ECCLESIASTES 7:8 CEV

Horse showing was not available to me in my younger years. Recently, being halfway to life expectancy, I was presented with an opportunity to carriage drive my horse in competition. This was not something I had ever considered, and quite frankly, neither had my aged horse. I invested a good year into getting ready for our first big day of showing, and despite my secret urge to toss in the reins at every discouraging moment of training, I pressed on. We took third on show day—and that was out of three entries. Although we came in last, by the end of it all we had achieved something that not everyone is able to do: we finished well.

In everything we do, whether we choose it or not, there is a finish point. Although it's nice to start well, what's more important is that we end well—and that means trusting God's wisdom all the way to the finish line.

We don't need to win or even meet our goals, but by finishing the task without giving up, we accomplish something great. In Hebrews 12:1, the apostle Paul said, "Let us run with perseverance the race marked out for us."

What task or calling has God set for you? Don't give up until He says it's complete. When we are in fellowship with God, the end of everything is better than the beginning. It's our commission to finish well.

....

Lord, I want to finish well. Help me to press on and never give up. Bless my steps and my steadfast effort, amen.

98

LIGHT UP THE WORLD

As he was getting into the boat, the man who had been possessed by demons begged him that he might be with him. But Jesus refused, and said to him, "Go home to your friends, and tell them how much the Lord has done for you, and what mercy he has shown you."
MARK 5:18–19 NRSV

My life with horses has been a slow but consistent one. In a twinkling moment in childhood, I decided I loved these amazing creatures. Although I have not always owned one, horses have had a presence in my life ever since. There are other horse people who fell in love with owning horses later in life, and they have a unique appreciation for these beautiful animals.

Our Christian testimonies can look the same way. There are those who have given their lives to Christ in childhood and those of us who have experienced dramatic conversions as adults. But it doesn't matter if our testimonies are slow-burning embers or roaring forest fires. What is important is that we share our faith with others.

Every fire needs a spark to set it off. And your story may be the spark that lights up the faith of the next big evangelist. I have a friend who owns and operates an equestrian academy. This academy brings God's gift of horses to kids who may not be able to afford them. My friend's mission field is dirty, fly infested, and full of teenagers who bring with them a lot of drama. But by her obedience, she might just be influencing the next Billy Graham or Beth Moore.

Whatever your testimony, the enemy is standing by to extinguish your flame. Don't let him douse it. The next time you feel as if you have nothing good to share, tell the world what Jesus has done for you. Light it up for the Lord.

....

Lord, help me to never shrink back from sharing my faith. Give me the courage to be Your witness and to light up the world, amen.

99

The Source of Truth

For the word of God is alive and active.
Hebrews 4:12

In ancient times, people didn't have devices to measure their horses, so they used something that was always available to them: their hands. A *hand* is still the unit of measurement for horses today, with one hand being equal to four inches.

In this day in which science and Google often replace the Bible as our standard measuring devices for truth, we are left to ponder whether we can believe in a creator or not. Sadly, because of misinformation, people are in danger of missing heaven by only twelve inches, which is roughly the distance between our hearts and our brains. While our hearts long for a relationship with God, our minds struggle with reason versus faith.

Although faith does play a role in the life of a Christian, so does thinking, and when we seek out answers to biblical questions, we strengthen our relationship with our Savior even in our doubts. While the Internet—and scientific discoveries—are a great source of truth up to a point, they fall short of being the standard. Prioritizing these sources over the Word of God is just like using only our hands to measure our horses: it can give us conflicting answers about their true height.

The Bible is reliable and relevant for living today. Consider the possibility that God has given us wisdom to meet every need and speak to even contemporary problems. Next time you feel confused about an issue or controversy, study what the Bible says, and ask the Holy Spirit to reveal God's heart to you. Then take a humble *and* unbiased approach to researching what scholars and theologians say on the issue.

Eventually, your heart and your mind will tell you that God's Word is our only standard for truth. His is the only measuring stick that really matters.

Lord, I want to measure spiritual issues by the standards of the Bible. Teach me, guide me, and help me to grow in truth, amen.

100

FROM DEATH TO LIFE

"Where, O death, is your victory? Where, O death, is your sting?"
The sting of death is sin, and the power of sin is the law. But thanks
be to God! He gives us the victory through our Lord Jesus Christ.
1 CORINTHIANS 15:55–57

When my feet are in the wrong place, my horse will let me know it. I have had my toes stepped on numerous times. The pain always reminds me of how heavy horses are and how dangerous working with them can be.

When the Bible steps on our feet by addressing a sin we are afraid to confront or give up, we are reminded of how heavy our sins can be. After accepting Christ in our hearts, the battle for our souls may be over, but the sting of sin will continue to harass us. However, God's Word can also remind us about what Christ's death on the cross has accomplished for us.

Years ago, I thought I was too far gone, and I not only had disappointed God but also was not worth bothering with anymore. The heaviness of sin and the fear of death nearly overwhelmed me. I couldn't understand how anyone, let alone God, could love me. As I was trying to figure things out, I viewed the movie *The Passion of the Christ*. I was completely awakened to the possibility that it was not too late for me when Jesus said, "Father, forgive them, for they do not know what they are doing" (Luke 23:34). He was offering me forgiveness; I just needed to reach out and take it.

Jesus gives us something we do not deserve because He loves us. His sacrifice frees us from the weight of sin and death. We just need to accept it. And if we understand what He did, then we are willing to change our ways. Now I get up every day and live my life appreciating His gift—the gift He had been trying to give me since birth, the gift I kept avoiding. I know I am forgiven, and God is enough.

Are you feeling burdened by sin? Has the Word stepped on your toes? Don't get caught up in regret or self-loathing. Confess what you've done, and then reach out and take His forgiveness. Grab hold of the eternal life He promises. In Christ, we are no longer afraid of death and no longer bound by sin. We are free!

....

Lord, through the death and resurrection of Jesus, I'm no longer afraid of the consequences of my sin or the reality of death. I praise You for this amazing truth, amen.